T0165773

Fast into the Night

FAST
into the
NIGHT

A WOMAN, HER DOGS, AND THEIR JOURNEY
NORTH ON THE IDITAROD TRAIL

Debbie Clarke Moderow

Library of Congress Cataloging-in-Publication Data
Moderow, Debbie Clarke.
Fast into the night : a woman, her dogs, and their journey north on the Iditarod Trail
    / Debbie Clarke Moderow.
LCCN 2015017310 | ISBN 978-1-59709-976-9 (pbk : alk paper) |
    ISBN 978-1-59709-908-0 (ebook)
1. Moderow, Debbie Clarke. 2. Iditarod (Race) 3. Sled dog racing—Alaska. 4. Women
mushers—Alaska—Biography. 5. Mushers—Alaska—Biography.
I. Title. SF440.15.M62 2016 | 798.8'3092—dc23
LC record available at https://lccn.loc.gov/2015017310

The National Endowment for the Arts, the Los Angeles County Arts Commission,
the Ahmanson Foundation, the Dwight Stuart Youth Fund, the Max Factor Family
Foundation, the Pasadena Tournament of Roses Foundation, the Pasadena Arts &
Culture Commission and the City of Pasadena Cultural Affairs Division, the City of
Los Angeles Department of Cultural Affairs, the Audrey & Sydney Irmas Charitable
Foundation, the Kinder Morgan Foundation, the Allergan Foundation, the Riordan
Foundation, and the Amazon Literary Partnership partially support Red Hen Press.

Second Edition
Published by Boreal Books
an imprint of Red Hen Press
www.borealbooks.org
www.redhen.org

For Juliet and Sydney,
my leaders on and off the trail,
and for Mark,
always willing us onward

Debbie with Juliet and Sydney, winter 2005

Contents

PART 2

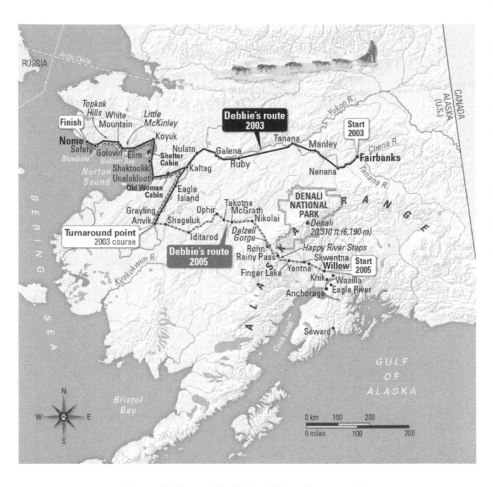

Map of Iditarod Trail Sled Dog Race routes,
2003 and 2005

Part 1

To see far is one thing, going there is another.
—CONSTANTIN BRANCUSI

Ready to go

1

Night Fog

Juliet and Kanga watch me. Standing in lead at the front of the line, they turn and follow me with their eyes as I step onto the runners of my dogsled. For the past fifteen minutes they've been clamoring to go—yapping and singing for the night trail and the star-speckled sky. Now they tremble with quiet anticipation. They know I'm about to reach for the rope and set us free.

"Good girls," I say. "Ready?"

I grab the end of the slipknot. Give it a tug. Juliet and Kanga leap, and so do the others. My ten huskies and I streak from camp in bright moonlight, slipping through shadows of gangly black spruce that line the outgoing trail.

For the first time all season conditions are perfect for mushing. It's ten degrees below zero with eight inches of fresh snow. A big round moon lights the trail and lightens my spirits, but I cannot ignore the weight of my plan. Iditarod starts in six short weeks, and training has been miserable all winter. To ask these dogs for another fifty-five miles after a six-hour rest seems like a lot, but I have to try it. It's time to make sure we're ready.

As we sweep around a wide bend toward the river, I study each dog's gait to make sure no one is sore. Shining my head lamp toward their feet, paw by moving paw I double-check that every bootie is on. I'm pleased that Kanga's new harness fits well, and that Nacho runs with focus next to his buddy Teton. Young Sydney prances with spunk; her ears are frisky tall. I'm so consumed with my huskies, I don't notice the wall of fog until we run right into it.

Ice crystals sting my eyes; the bright beam of my head lamp illuminates a mass of ice flecks. As the dogs accelerate, threads of silver rush toward me in a blinding onslaught. I struggle to see where we're going, but they aren't bothered. Bounding into the glitter, Juliet woofs and noses Kanga, who responds with a happy-dog shake on the run. No one misses a stride.

For the next hour and part of another, I shield my eyes with one hand and hold on to the handlebars with the other. Focusing on the dog team helps me ignore the fog, but after fifteen miles my eyes tire from the effort. I turn off my head lamp and run by feel.

It doesn't take long to adjust—and to notice moonbeams sifting through billows of haze. The resulting shadows threaten at first. We run toward dark shapes that look like moose and approach an expanse of bare ground that turns out to be an ice-fog mirage. With every mile my fears subside, and then I give in.

Losing myself to the huff of their breathing and their steady pull on the line, I stop trying to gauge our tempo or analyze whether one dog is loping instead of trotting. It doesn't matter if the trail ahead is strewn with rocks, and I no longer fret about what lurks in the willows.

My huskies and I cruise up and over those frosted hills for hours. As we move through murky light toward the faint glow of dawn, we share a primordial momentum. Although I cannot see them, at last I understand that they are ready.

Ready for Iditarod.

No matter how long the trail or how rough her conditions, I know we will go.

Kanga and Juliet lead Debbie and team onto the 2003 Iditarod Trail

2

Countdown

2003 Iditarod start: Fairbanks, Alaska. March 3, 11:00 AM

Sixteen huskies donning crimson harnesses charge into the chute. Four officials grab the bulging dogsled to make sure the team stays anchored for the two-minute countdown. Overhead, small planes arc in a bright March sky; the *thwap* of a helicopter blends with the buzz of fans cheering and of dogs yapping and yowling. Barricades line the outgoing trail, and throngs of people lean over them. Watching, waiting.

This is an annual ritual. I know it well. The sight of courageous Iditarod mushers and their canine athletes launching onto the one-thousand-mile trail usually casts me into a tearful state of awe. But I'm not crying now. The romantic in me had better not engage. I'm the small woman wearing bib #32, the musher who has just ridden the sled runners into the chute. After years of preparation, I'm the Iditarod rookie fighting for composure, seeking focus in a windstorm of hype.

The voice in my busy head speaks: *It's only about the dogs.*

So I look to them, to my sixteen beauties with their glossy fur and feathered tails, paired on the long line ahead of me. They're a rowdy bunch—barking and leaping—crazed with impatience for the trail. My husband, Mark, stands with the dogs, trying to calm them; so do our grown children, Andy and Hannah. The four of us have negotiated many race starts over the past fifteen years, most often for the kids. But this countdown is different, and we all know it. I need to pay attention.

"We got 'em, Debbie. Your rig isn't goin' anywhere. Feel free to get on up there with your team," the official tells me.

I nod and step off the runners. That's when I notice the clusters of school kids holding signs and calling my name. Their rosy cheeks and busy voices shout high expectations. These children believe in me. The mere hint that I'm their hero spins everything out of control. My stomach lurches and the snow beneath my feet rolls like a wave. I have to find my way to my huskies.

In two strides I'm with Zeppelin and his sweetheart, Fire. Running in wheel position, they're responsible for keeping the sled clear of trees and other obstacles. Strong and agile, Zeppy is my rascal black-and-white hound dog. His floppy black ears frame an innocent gaze that doesn't fool me today. Without my friend kneeling next to him, holding him by the harness, he'd be chewing up the gang line. She scratches him behind the ears, and for the moment he behaves. Meanwhile, mellow Fire nuzzles my leg and looks at me with sweet adoration. Her light-blue eyes promise that everything will be fine. She's been to Nome several times with other mushers; I've paired her with Zeppy hoping she'll be a good mentor. I coo at Fire, give Zeppy a stern hello, and then move on to Piney and Creek, who lean against each other wagging their tails. Creek is so bulked up this season, I call her my little bowling ball. I put my hands on either side of her face and look into her zany eyes—one blue and the other brown. Sweet Piney is jealous and nips my leg. I answer by shaking her paw.

Next are skinny-boy Nacho and the ever-focused Lil' Su, two of Andy's charges. They leap and bark while he stands smiling alongside them. I greet these spicy teammates before embracing my twenty-year-old son.

"You can do this, Mom," he tells me. Andy should know—he's the most experienced musher in the family. I pull him into a hug, as if to absorb some of his brassy nerve. If it weren't for him, I would never be here. His words make me stand a little bit taller, and for the moment my jitters subside.

It's hard to believe I've greeted six dogs and am not even halfway through the lineup. I usually train an eight-dog team—plenty of power, yet manageable. This sixty-five-foot gang line looks endless, and I know the whiplash at tight corners could send all 120 pounds of me flying. For the past week I've considered starting with fourteen dogs, but one thousand miles is a long way. During the race, mushers can drop dogs—leave anyone who is sore or simply not having fun in the care of veterinarians before flying home—but substitutions aren't allowed. Despite the potential for too much power, it's best to start with sixteen.

Taiga and Spot are next. They greet me with wiggles, Spot with a rising howl. Taiga, the strawberry-blond princess of the team, leans against me at the perfect angle for a butt scratch. When I comply she shifts contentedly from side to side. Meanwhile her sidekick, our all-white Spot, woofs and wags, playing the crowd. Mark keeps watch over these two. He gathers me into his arms.

"See you in Nome," he jokes.

"Think again," I respond. "You'd better be in Nenana." He knows full well that this isn't good-bye, and that he'll see me later today at the first roadside checkpoint.

He smiles and squeezes my arm. Of course he'll be there.

Ahead of Mark stand Keno and Vickie. Keno, a princely red, white, and brown pinto, has fluffy white cheeks—perfect for grabbing in each hand while I tell him he's handsome. Now the sensitive boy is awash in nerves. As the loudspeaker crackles with static, Keno's lower jaw trembles, mirroring the anxious part of myself I'm trying to tame. I want to console him, but a pat on the head is all I can muster before hurrying on to girls Teton and Strider. I kneel next to them, and they both lick my face. Blond Teton gets carried away and tackles me with affection. She almost knocks me over. I stand and pat sleek Strider before moving on to swing dogs Sydney and Roulette.

Positioned behind the leaders, swing dogs play an important guiding role at the front of a team. Often leaders-in-training, they possess a calm and steady drive. Sydney is barely two, the youngster on the team. Red with white trim, she has a short, adorable nose. There's no question she wins the beauty-queen title in our kennel. When I say hello she paws the air and lowers her head in a coy canine curtsy. I rub her shoulders and Roulette's, hoping to soothe my own jagged nerves. Then in one step I'm with leaders Kanga and Juliet.

Iditarod leaders are a talented lot. These are the confident heroes who delight in catching the first whiff of the trail. They act as trail guides for the others behind them, reveling in the challenge of route finding. I've carefully chosen Kanga and Juliet to lead us over our first Iditarod miles.

There are additional leaders on the line: Taiga and Lil' Su, as well as some others. Because Kanga has done this before, she's my pick for steadying the long line during starting-day hype. She's an Iditarod veteran who I bought as a four-year-old in order to ground my rookie team with some wisdom. Muscled and compact, Kanga is a serious brown girl with tan trim. She is the alpha of our kennel and bears a scar on her lip from an altercation with a former teammate. Kanga is all power—and usually gets her way. I'm heartened that she knows more about Iditarod than I do.

In contrast, Juliet is my playful Tinker Bell. She's the whimsical cheerleader, my tiny gray spitfire who runs up front with a lighthearted disposition. She loves starting lines so much that she works herself into a state of ecstasy—biting the snow, gurgling with anticipation, and spinning with glee for the upcoming trail. Once under way she motors along with a spunky trot. Kanga's wisdom coupled with Juliet's spirit should be perfect for this first sixty-five-mile run.

Hannah has raced these two in lead often, so she's proud to watch over them now. When I kneel to pat Juliet, she ricochets out of Hannah's arms and pounces back to play with Sydney. Familiar with Juliet's antics, my daughter is quick to respond. She reels in our rambunctious little leader and steadies her in place alongside Kanga the Magnificent, who poses like a statue fixated on the trail. When I lay my hand on Kanga's back she gives my arm a quick affectionate nip.

Aware that the countdown is nearing, I hug Hannah. Then Andy comes to our side and we share a three-way embrace. I tell them how good this all feels, but really I'm posing as an upbeat mom. More than anything I don't want my children to worry. There's a chance they won't be at the first checkpoint, Nenana, because of their flight back to college. This might be our final good-bye. I cling to them for a few more seconds, and when I let go, I look to my leaders. They draw me in.

"Good girls, Kanga and Juliet. Are you ready? We're going to Nome," I say. Juliet wiggles and tries to snatch the hat off my head. The crowd roars, and Kanga jerks against the line. I'm patting her, trying to reassure her, when a large presence looms and a strong hand grabs my shoulder.

"Debbie, that's enough." In his baritone voice, race marshal Mark Nordman continues, "Go to your sled. *Now!*"

He reiterates what is obvious to my huskies and hundreds of people watching: our countdown is past. Evidently the dogs were making so much noise that I didn't hear the words "Five . . . four . . . three . . . two . . . one . . . go!" Or maybe I'm just oblivious. Either way, I've managed to miss my own Iditarod start.

I run to my sled, past laughing volunteers. When one of the sled holders asks me if I'm ready, I say no but realize that it doesn't matter. He pulls my snow hook anchor as I step onto the runners, and before I can draw half a breath, the dogs charge and the sled rockets forward. The power of sixteen is something I've never felt before.

A series of expletives spew from my mouth—that's what I'm told later by friends watching. My heavy sled lurches to the side into a deep cockeyed rut where thirty-one mushers have stood on their brakes ahead of me. Somehow I manage to hang on and stay upright, resisting gravity's pull. Then, with both feet on the drag, I slow the dogs to a manageable pace. The air cools my face, and there's panting and the rhythm of sixty-four paws on snow. Dog collars jingle and well-wishers, standing in clusters along the trail, cheer us on our way.

The 2003 Iditarod start is hardly what I've imagined. That we leave the line a few seconds late is not the only race-day surprise. We aren't at the traditional starting line just north of Anchorage, and it isn't the first Sunday in March. Instead, the 2003 Iditarod begins on a Monday, 350 miles north of Anchorage in Fairbanks. The rivers in Southcentral Alaska never froze up during this warm winter, so two weeks before race day, organizers were forced to come up with an alternate route. We'll follow the Chena, Tanana, Nenana, and Yukon Rivers for seven hundred miles before joining the traditional Iditarod Trail in Kaltag, some three hundred miles from Nome.

This "river race," as it will come to be called, is unprecedented in Iditarod's thirty-year history—the result of a bizarre warm season. Snow came so late, we were still training the dogs in front of a four-wheeler ATV at Thanksgiving. When Andy and Hannah returned home for Christmas, we managed to sled on a skim of snow, but only for a few short miles. In early January the rains returned and trail conditions deteriorated. A pilot friend who had flown over the trail described the mountainous section as a dangerous mess of rock and ice. That's when I called Andy and warned him I might pull out of the race.

"I just don't know if I'm strong enough," I told him. "If I can't control the sled, I have no business taking the dogs out there."

"Don't give me that," my son replied with a snap. "One good blizzard could fix everything. You can't just change your mind now, Mom. You know you want to run Iditarod."

I told him that of course I did. And I do. When you sign up for Iditarod in midsummer, you commit to yourself and everyone else that on the first weekend of March you'll head out on the one-thousand-mile trail to Nome. No matter what. You and your dogs will make the best of what you're granted. But I also told Andy that my first responsibility was to Juliet and Kanga, Lil' Su, and the others. To keep them happy and healthy would always override my tough-Iditarod-girl persona. I was determined, even if it meant withdrawing from this year's race, to keep my promise to them.

The dogs have always been the real Iditarod heroes. I've known that ever since March 1980 when I went to an Iditarod start for the first time. Despite the human hoopla—the champions giving interviews,

the press shooting photos, the children all bundled up waiting for autographs—I saw only the dogs.

They left a lasting impression, those bulked-up Alaskan huskies of
all colors and sizes. Some had blue eyes, others brown. A few looked like
Labradors, while many resembled the furry pointed-ear malamutes in
movies about early Arctic expeditions. These athletes stood patiently
as people strapped colorful booties on their paws. Some yapped and
a few growled; many collaborated in song. Thousands of tails wagged.

Having grown up in the company of hunting dogs, I was drawn to
these iconic working canines of the north. I read all I could about these
magnificent huskies and learned they were mutts: glorious mixed-
breed working dogs instilled with a desire to run. Iditarod dogs were
descendants of huskies who had long lived and traveled across Alaska, first with Alaska Natives and later with gold prospectors and mail
drivers in the early twentieth century. Bred for teamwork demanded
by the northern trail, these dogs were devoted to one another—and to
their humans.

In 1973 the dog sledding tradition had inspired a man named Joe
Redington Sr. to create an event called the Iditarod Trail Sled Dog Race.
He wanted to honor Alaska's historic trail along with its canines. Seven
years later, when I first saw the huskies of Iditarod, I wanted to know
them better. Never did I imagine that within a decade, a backyard dog
team would claim our young family's heart.

At the end of my phone call with Andy, just six weeks ago, I told
him I would postpone withdrawing from Iditarod but under no circumstances would I take our huskies on a trail too rough for me to
handle. Our conversation had helped me regain my focus, but in the
end it was Mark who settled my nerves.

My husband insisted that the dogs and I move north to our cabin in Denali Park, where temperatures were cooler. He proposed that I train the team full-time, living and breathing only for them. Meanwhile, he would stay in our Anchorage home and focus on a multitude of race chores. He'd oversee dog food preparation for the trail, gathering and bagging everything from kibble to beef, sausage, and salmon. He promised to reinforce my sled for the roughest conditions and work on a new, tougher drag to slow the sled. Mark vowed to do all this during the week in his nonworking hours. On weekends he'd join us in Denali.

Mark figured Spot's song for the trail, Kanga's nip on my arm, Lil' Su's leaping in harness, would reignite my determination, and he was right. Between mid-January and race day I immersed myself in the mushing lifestyle like I never had before. The dogs' day was my own, beginning with 5:00 AM feedings when they yowled and danced for their ladleful of hot steaming breakfast—and ending with the midnight howls that we shared after I doled out fresh straw. During those weeks in Denali we increased the runs from twenty to fifty-five miles. On weekends Mark and I took them camping.

Now, speeding away from the Iditarod start, I'm riding the runners behind a dog team that has already pulled me to a new understanding of myself. After a season of challenge, and the resolution that finally came, we've been granted a lucky break. The last-minute course change means there will be no mountain crossing. This is the only Iditarod in the race's thirty-year history whose teams won't have to negotiate the Happy River Steps or the other drop-offs in the Alaska Range. This 2003 course features mellow river travel. It's the perfect route for me and my dogs.

As we cruise on a packed snow-covered trail—the best we've seen all winter—I'm aware that we've already accomplished a lot. Fifteen hundred hard-earned training miles are behind us. Provisions for me and the dogs have been sent ahead in drop bags to twenty-two checkpoints. After months of intense anticipation, the multitude of what-ifs no longer matters. The trail, the weather, the dogs' fitness and mine—they are what they are.

Even our goal is simple: to reach Nome with healthy dogs wagging their tails. A laminated schedule inside my pocket details our run-rest plan. It's conservative, while holding us to a consistent steady tempo. A digital watch duct-taped to my handlebar reminds me to keep track of the time.

Now the pull of my powerful team takes me past the scrubby brush on the banks of the Chena River—away from the dull ache of the empty nest, the expectations of the screaming crowd, and the nagging doubt in my own abilities. Now that my huskies and I are moving, I can accept the notion that we're heading into a wilderness topography over which we have little control. All I can do—and what I must do—is focus on the dogs out front and the trail underfoot.

We're on our way.

Do Clarke on the step of her autogiro

3

Beginnings

When I was a child in southern Connecticut, my parents never imagined that one day I'd run a dog team across Alaska. Nor could I have foreseen moving three thousand miles away from the red clapboard house with white trim that sat on top of a hill beneath the towering oak, on the edge of the woods where Mom and I planted daffodils— and Dad and I searched every spring for trout lilies. My mother and father would never have predicted I'd live in a distant corner of North America, far from southern Vermont where together we skied in winter and fly-fished the Battenkill and Mettawee Rivers in summer. But they shouldn't have been completely surprised. It was from my parents that I learned to take on life's dares.

My mother was a daddy's girl. Born to a gentle Episcopalian mother and a wild-man father, she was the first of three daughters. Her father was an early aviator, and Mom eagerly assumed his airborne spirit. By the time she met my dad, not only had she flown her floatplane under the Brooklyn Bridge, she'd flown her Fairchild up and down the Atlantic coastline, winging her way to glamorous events including the Kentucky Derby. Her debutante photo shows her standing on the step of her autogiro wearing a leather helmet and a mink jacket. Birthed into opportunity, my mother never let social convention get in her way. She chased down adventure. Mom knew where she wanted to go.

When they met, my father was surely smitten with Mom's valiant style. Like his future bride, Dad reached for life's fun. He was an accomplished college gymnast, and during my parents' courtship he allegedly showed off by walking across creeks on his hands. For a wedding present, he gave Mom a sixteen-gauge shotgun. Together they trained English setters and hunted for grouse and woodcock in thickets of bittersweet and New England brambles. They fly-fished for brown trout and brookies in the waters of upstate New York with handcrafted bamboo rods and flies tied with feathers from chickens raised in their backyard. Always ribbing each other, neither failed to notice who caught the largest trout.

Mom and Dad had recently married when World War II began. Like many in their generation, my father quickly enlisted. When he was sent to the front lines of battle in North Africa and Italy, he left behind my mother, their young son, and a soon-to-be-born daughter. Mom nearly died giving birth to my sister, but she managed to survive. So did my father, eventually rising to the level of captain.

Decades later, I asked him what it was like to take part in combat. Dad didn't want to talk about the fighting. He looked away, took a deep breath, and said that sometimes bad things happen—that you need to do your best and move on. On the topic of his military accomplishments, he insisted that rank was highly overrated. "I was no goddamn better than the lowliest soldier," he told me.

My brother and sister were thirteen and fourteen when I was born. I was the lucky one, welcomed into strong arms of older parents who had weathered the war and created a stable life when it ended. Throughout my childhood I was Mom and Dad's eager sidekick—camping, fishing, skiing, and hiking. When I turned thirteen they took me west to the CM Ranch, for the very first time.

My parents had worked on a Wyoming dude ranch in their twenties. Decades later they celebrated returning to the high sagebrush country of their youth. Together that summer we trotted quarter horses named Bowie and Sable and Keno on trails that twisted through sandstone badlands. We went on a pack trip to a wilderness area on the crest of the Continental Divide, where we loped through meadows of paintbrush, larkspur, and lupine. Following Mom and Dad on horseback was to assume their delight for trails that linked one wide alpine valley to the next. This spirited place nourished my parents' dreams and jump-started mine.

One day when we were out on a guest ride, the head wrangler, Greg, circled back alongside my father and said, "Hey, ole Lew, you want to race?" Spitting his Copenhagen chew off to the side of his saddle, he pointed to a long flat sandy plateau just ahead. Dad's eyes widened, and for a moment he was silent.

Then the cowboy spoke again. "You know what they say: No guts, no glory."

My father, well aware of General George S. Patton's famous line, smiled wide and responded, "Goddamnit, ole Greg. Let's go!"

There were other guests and cowboys on the ride. We all knew this was hardly a safe or standard proposition, but in my father Greg saw a kindred spirit. He pulled the brim of his black cowboy hat down on his forehead and told us all to wait. Then he and my father took off in a dusty, hoof-pounding gallop.

Within a few minutes they returned trotting side by side: a lawyer from New England and a Wyoming cowboy, bound by an old-fashioned dare. I knew right then this would not be our last visit to Wyoming.

Ten years after that first trip out west, I left my New England home to settle there. I'd recently graduated from Princeton and worked as a paralegal for a major law firm housed high in Manhattan's Rockefeller Center. The prestige was flattering and the pay generous, but the lure of the city did nothing to temper my longing for the sandy sagebrush hills, the open sky that pledged possibility, and the seasons that kept ranchers honest. So in 1978 I moved to Sheridan, Wyoming, intending to stay. I planned to attend law school eventually, in order to acquire skills to help protect the wild places I'd come to cherish.

It was the next summer, in 1979, when a smoke jumper boyfriend and I were invited to Alaska to take part in a mountain-climbing expedition. Just a few weeks before we were to fly north, he canceled—from the expedition as well as the romance. Any disappointment of mine was overshadowed by determination; no one would take away my chance to visit one of the wildest places on the planet. So I headed to Alaska by myself, intent upon seeing the glaciers, climbing the peaks, and experiencing the midnight sun. It felt fine to visit on my own.

Jim and Roni Hale, the expedition leaders, met me in Anchorage's small but crowded airport. I remember gritty-looking travelers, many toting fishing rods or guns—and even a few with skis. There were swarms of bearded men, clusters of people wearing matching oil-company jackets, and an enormous mounted grizzly bear that leered at me in a snarl.

After leading me through the busy terminal to the car, Jim explained, "We're off to a weekly get-together of climbers. It's hosted by our friend Markie—famed backcountry skier and lawyer extraordinaire."

Within five minutes I walked through Mark's door. Lively conversation filled his spacious living room. The smell of grilled hot dogs wafted among a friendly beer-drinking crowd. I remember several people studying a topo map spread out on a large table, and a tall fellow describing his recent climb of an unnamed peak. There was a border collie milling around, and a white fluffy pup named Tuna Fish.

The party spilled into every corner of the condo. As I wandered from room to room I noticed Mark talking to some friends in the bathroom, of all places. The counter was crammed with bottles; he'd just brewed a fresh batch of beer. Across the hall in a small bedroom with drawn curtains, a subdued group watched slides of a recent rescue mission. I later learned that they had taken part in a high-stakes attempt to save some friends after they fell near the summit of a mountain called Carpathian. Mark and some other Alaska Rescue Group volunteers reached the climbers only to discover that no one had survived. During the subsequent body recovery, they endured a life-threatening storm. Eventually a harrowing ride in a helicopter delivered them to safety.

"The weather up there was wicked," Mark explained. "The whole situation was rough, but we had to go there. Someone had to get their bodies off that mountain."

The gathering that night ended early. These were people who lived for wilderness, and they all had weekend ambitions. As the guests began to leave, I looked for Mark. I wanted to thank this bearded man with the bright blue eyes for a fine Alaskan welcome.

When I found him in the kitchen, we exchanged a few pleasantries. Then Mark's border collie, trained for avalanche rescue, trotted to his side. "Want to see something?" Mark asked me. Without waiting for my response, he addressed his dog: "Hamish," he said, "would you rather be married or dead?"

Hamish rolled onto his back. His head lolled limp to the side, while his lifeless furry paws folded neatly above his fluffy white belly. Jim and a few others groaned—they'd obviously seen this trick a few times before. I didn't recognize it at the time, but the dog and his human had issued an irresistible challenge.

Basking in the flair of his own making, Mark proceeded to ask Jim what we were doing the following day. Jim responded that we'd buy food for our trip in the morning, pack provisions and gear in the afternoon, and attend church at night. Mark raised his eyebrows and looked for my reaction. He claims he detected a wince.

"She didn't come all the way up here to go to church. I'll show her a good time." The attorney mountain climber in red soccer shorts and his Celestial Seasonings T-shirt made a good guess. I wasn't going to fall for another romance, but I had even less motivation to attend church. I figured there was nothing to lose.

Our first date started with the movie *Alien,* after which we went to a bar called Chilkoot Charlie's. I would learn later that "Koots" was the rough-and-tumble frontier-town establishment, notorious for all sorts of trouble, but I was oblivious at the time. I remember sitting on tall bar stools. Flirtatious conversation about mountains and dogs and unclimbed Alaskan peaks. Wood shavings covered the floor, and a peddler walked table to table selling flowers. Mark bought me a long-stemmed red rose.

It must have been close to midnight when we stepped out of Chilkoot's into the glowing light of sunset. Before going back to Jim's house, we drove to an overlook above Anchorage, where we admired Denali's slate-blue silhouette as it darkened against the tangerine sky. Bathed in the soft light of the midnight sun, Mark took my hands and pronounced he'd join our five-person expedition the following week.

"Don't you ever work?" I asked, well aware that lawyers could be a lot of talk and no action.

"Work?" he teased. "Oh that's just something I do on the side."

I told him I wouldn't believe him until a plane circled above our camp.

At noon the next day a ski plane deposited our expedition—me, Jim and Roni, and two of their friends—in a snowbound glacial valley in the heart of the Alaska Range. There, at the edge of the blue-ice Ruth Glacier, we set up base camp. Granite peaks named Dickey, Barille, and Moose's Tooth surrounded our three little tents. At first the massive amphitheater unnerved me. It took more than a few hours to adjust to the notion that we amounted to temporary specks in an ageless topography of snow, ice, and rock.

For three days the weather was clear. Roped together on skis, we traversed high mountain passes and navigated glaciers that encircled Denali, North America's tallest peak. On day four, the wind picked up; eventually a ceiling of clouds settled beneath the summits. Grounded in soggy tents, we were enveloped in dense August fog. Avalanches fell in zinging free falls from cornices melting overhead. We played card games and ate mac and cheese, pilot biscuits, and Snickers bars. The two fellows and I read one another's books and tried to be patient, while Jim and Roni spent long hours in their tent reading scripture. Our group was in no immediate danger, but I couldn't help feeling cheated to be holed up during my brief Alaskan adventure.

Finally, on day six, a breeze rustled our tent and brilliant sunlight brightened its orange nylon walls. As the five of us celebrated over oatmeal and Tang, we planned a ski jaunt. In the midst of our talking logistics, something buzzed overhead. The sound was faint at first, and then it grew louder.

I peered outside and spotted a white plane on skis flying just above us. Roni wondered if we were being picked up early. She might not have known that Mark wanted to join us, but my heart lurched at the possibility. As the plane descended I saw two figures inside it. Then an object with streamers tumbled onto the ground. I scrambled across the snowfield to investigate, picking up a beer can decorated with surveyor tape streamers. A handwritten note was duct-taped to its side: *Dear cute girl from Wyoming, get your rope and take me home. Your pal, Mark.*

The Taylorcraft landed on a makeshift "airstrip" we'd skied the day before. As the pilot cut the engine, he waved to Jim; then the door opened and a passenger jumped out. Mark tossed his heavy pack, a neatly coiled climbing rope, skis, poles, and a pile of climbing hardware onto the snow. After acknowledging the others with a nod, the knickered attorney threw me into a ballroom dip, gave me a kiss, and moved into my tent. We've called each other home ever since.

Debbie and Kanga

4

Open Water

Iditarod day 1: Nenana

It's late evening on Iditarod start day. Our five-hour rest in Nenana is over, and we're ready to leave. I'm standing on the runners, wishing the dogs would calm down. You would think they'd be settled after the sixty-five-mile run here, but they're all wound up, yapping and yowling to the crowd watching and the moon rising. It's time to get back under way.

Nenana is normally a sleepy little town, but not tonight. Due to Iditarod's reroute, sixty-five teams are passing through in quick succession. Hundreds of race fans have driven here to cheer mushers on their way. Local volunteers scurry around, welcoming the crowd and helping teams in and out.

The people of Nenana are honored to host a checkpoint on Iditarod; their community of several hundred played a pivotal role in Alaska's dogsledding history. This is the legendary place where, in 1925, the well-known relay of serum began. At the train station just one block from my dog team, the first of twenty mushers received the package of serum and set out with his dog team toward Nome, where children were dying of a deadly diphtheria outbreak.

Now, seventy-eight years later, it's our time to head to Nome—and my huskies know it. As their excitement rises, so do my fears. It's almost too much to consider, the departure into the night. So I look to Mark for one last smile. Then, just as I reach for my snow hook anchor to set us free, someone runs toward me waving.

"Stop!" he shouts. "Stay right there—you need to wait. We've got a problem."

At first I only want to argue. It's after 9:00 PM, daylight is long gone, and I'm scared of leaving checkpoints in the dark. We should be able to go whenever we're ready, but before I can object, a voice crackles on his radio.

"Okay, here's the deal. The river's breaking up. There's an open lead that crosses the trail. We're working on setting markers around it. Don't let anyone go. Did you get that? Over."

The river's breaking up.

The words stun. I'm suffering a relapse of start-line worry, fretting that this dog team is too powerful, the icy trail too rough, and the miles to Nome too many. This is, after all, the real leaving—the point at which we're fully committed. Now the anxious voice in my head, the one only I can hear, screams.

Really? We're to embark on this adventure of a lifetime skirting open water? In the dark? With sixteen dogs?

My huskies are oblivious to the danger. Paired on the line, they're certain that in one glorious second we will be on our way. Tonight's leader, Lil' Su, is leaping high in the air; alongside her Taiga circles in place. Sensing imminent adventure, swing dog Juliet is nothing short of ecstatic; she backs up and tries to bound ahead, then chews on the line as if it's a bone. Next to her, Sydney wiggles in glee. No voice on the radio will worry them, and right now nothing will alter their focus. I want to feel an ounce of their joy, but I only imagine river water.

"Easy, Juliet. Take it easy, girls," I beg. I'm walking pair to pair, trying to calm them, when the official's radio crackles again.

"Okay, tell Debbie she's good to go."

That message stops me from taking another step.

Right.

A few minutes ago there was an open lead, and now I'm "good to go"? *What sort of wisdom plays into that green light?*

As if he can read my mind, Mark walks swiftly alongside me. He's trying to tell me something, but I talk first. "What are the chances they've rerouted far enough from the lead?" I ask.

I'm seeking collaboration in my fright, but my husband just looks away.

The official responds, "No worries, honey, we got you going around it."

I don't believe him. If other teams have already run over ice that's broken up, what will keep my dogs from following their scent? That's what dog teams do—they follow tracks of the teams ahead.

I'm reeling with panic when a fellow walks up and announces that he and some others have come to help us get out. Then Mark grabs my shoulders, and his eyes bore into mine. He tells me I'll be just fine.

"Are you sure?" I ask this man who understands that my inner compass seeks adventure but can swing easily toward an opposing pole of debilitating doubt.

"Keep your chin up and your head down," he answers.

Then he tells me he knows I can do this and gives me a brief, tight hug. For a moment—when he lets go—I believe him.

I stride toward my sled, past the long line of dogs. Somewhere in my peripheral vision is my older sister, Vicky, who's flown in from Connecticut. She hastily throws her arms around me and tries to choke back tears. Off to the side I notice my physical trainer, who's come for the send-off yet understands little about mushing. Bewildered, he does the only thing he knows to do in time of trial: he bows his head in prayer.

I have no time for tears or prayer. I'm thinking of Andy and Hannah when I step onto the runners—it's good they're already on the way back to college. For an instant I imagine Hannah's face, pale with fright for her rookie mother and dogs heading toward open water. In my mind Andy is irritating his sister by chattering optimism while masking his own fear.

One more time I cast off my mom persona and take my place on the runners. Then I gather my courage along with the snow hooks. Sensing an imminent launching, the dogs leap and yowl.

I nod to the five or six volunteers holding the gang line that I'm ready, and whisper, "Okay" to the team.

All sixteen bound ahead, while the volunteers hang on to the line and pull us wide around the building. As soon as we've cleared its corner, they let go. The line tightens with a snap and my huskies quiet. I'm standing with both feet on my brake behind a dog team charging into darkness. We barrel along an icy lane, past a blur of buildings and cars.

With a desperate deep voice that doesn't sound familiar, I beg, "Whooaaa."

My huskies don't consider slowing. Instead they launch over a snow berm and down a rocky bank, and within seconds they're galloping on ice smooth enough for skating. They move effortlessly in the narrow beam of my head lamp. I could illuminate a wider view of the river by turning my head, but I don't. If we're going past open water, I don't want to see it, and if we're running right for it, there is nothing I can do. I hold my breath and pump the brake—which slows the sled slightly and makes a screeching sound that encourages the dogs to run faster.

We reach the far side of that restless river in a matter of minutes, but it feels like forever. When the team scrambles up an icy bank and the sled ricochets around a tight, dark wooded corner, I exhale relief. As the long line of dogs weaves around hummocks and my elbows brush against branches of alders, the terror of our takeoff fades. We're traveling on solid ground.

Debbie and Mark skiing on the Ruth Glacier, summer 1979

5

A Cool, Dark Stillness

On August 19, 1979, the climbing expedition had ended, and my Alaskan vacation should have been over. This was the weekend I was scheduled to begin waitressing back home in Wyoming—to earn a few dollars before heading to law school. Instead, Mark and I walked along a forested trail and talked to imaginary bears.

"Hey, Bear," he said.

"Hi, Bear," I echoed.

The brush was thick alongside us, making visibility poor. Mark had explained that grizzlies often wandered the valley—feeding on soapberries or tender roots of willows. "The last thing we want to do is surprise one," he told me. The idea was to make lots of noise so they'd hear us and run off.

You'd think that as a newcomer to grizzly country I would have been nervous, but the possibility that we'd come upon such a creature thrilled me. I was a daring twenty-four-year old, infatuated with life's surprises. Now, instead of returning to my carefully orchestrated life in the Rockies, I was considering relocating to Alaska for a man.

That clear-sky morning presented itself like a gift. It felt like a childhood snow day, when I was supposed to be doing one thing and was granted an unexpected chance to do something else. The rumble of the nearby creek reminded me of the Catskill waters I'd fly-fished as soon as I was tall enough to wade. Even the smells of the trail enticed me. The unmistakable scent of ripening currants and musky frost-nipped leaves were signposts on the way to my favorite season: winter.

As I followed Mark along the trail, my thoughts jumped like stones skipping over glassy water—from bears munching on willows, to untracked ski slopes, then back to this man with a steady and confident step. After a while our traveling rhythm calmed my racing spirit. As the willows thinned and the sky broadened, we stopped to admire the craggy peaks that vaulted around us. Some mountains cradled snowfields on high slopes; others birthed waterfalls that spilled down rocky gullies to the lush green valley floor. I asked Mark to show me Byron—the peak we'd climb that day. He leaned close, pointed to the up-valley horizon, and described the route we would follow.

It all looked straightforward enough. In a mile or so we'd reach the glacier, then traverse the lower snowfield before ascending its left-hand edge to several moderate pitches. Following his description, I could make out a juncture higher up, where we'd get off the glacier and onto a rocky ridge that led to Byron's 4,700-foot summit.

I had never climbed such a spectacular mountain. My eyes lingered on her twin snowcapped peaks that posed like a sassy double dare. A high, gentle saddle lay between them. I remember imagining we'd walk that line—hand in hand along a tightrope that straddled this valley and the next. I asked Mark about the view. He described an endless expanse of unclimbed peaks. He said from Byron's summit we would look at glaciers that stretched for miles, all the way to the fjords off Prince William Sound.

August 19 had beckoned like a bright promise. In hindsight it's easy to spot danger lurking. Two weeks earlier, before Mark joined the expedition, our group had actually navigated the massive glaciated Ruth Gorge. I'd skied it roped between Jim and Roni, moving tentatively over narrow ice bridges and zipping over others translucent from thinning ice. Back at base camp I had remarked about the thrill of the traverse. My enthusiasm was met with cold stares.

"There was nothing good about it," Jim said.

Someone else told me that we had no business being there. I heard them and cringed, embarrassed to have been so naïve. Still, it had been spectacular to ski where few had ever gone—and we had gotten away with it.

Then, just the evening before the Byron climb, I'd gone with Mark to another Alaska Rescue Group barbecue. He and his ARG friends regularly practiced techniques to keep themselves and others out of harm's way. That night they gathered to drink a few beers and practice setting up a Z-pulley, useful in crevasse rescue. For one enlightened moment I recognized the importance of this skill.

"I know you've got this down," I said to Mark, "but what if we're climbing together and you're stuck in a crevasse? I don't know if I could set up a pulley by myself."

He assured me that of course I could but that it wouldn't be necessary. Then he added, "Besides, that's why Nick and Jill are coming with us tomorrow. There's safety in numbers."

The next morning we'd been walking for about a half hour when the trail ended and the snowfield began. We had agreed to wait there for Nick and Jill, who followed ten minutes behind us. No ordinary meeting place, this was the spot where the belly of the glacier formed a blue ice cavern that arced over the creek. Water rained from the cave's roof onto the pool below. Its surface twinkled like a constellation packed with too many stars.

When Nick and Jill arrived, we made a few jokes and snacked on jerky and trail mix. Then we all sat down and strapped crampons onto our boots. Their sharp points would enable us to walk safely on ice. We talked about not needing to rope up at first; the lower glacier was fairly flat, and this late in the summer its crevasses would be completely exposed and easy to walk around. We'd rope together in pairs when the grade steepened and the crevasses were covered with snow.

Mark and I were the first to head out; Nick and Jill followed a few minutes behind. I always loved that—being the first on the trail—to ski fresh tracks in new snow or to lope my quarter horse ahead of others over Wyoming's sage-covered hills. Mark walked in front of me that morning, and that made good sense. After all, this was his country, not mine. I'd only been on a glacier once before, during the recent expedition in the Alaska Range.

We moved easily past small crevasses, gray fissures in a wide white surface. I remember stopping to look back and admire the lush valley we'd traveled. Now I could see more: the massive flat-topped ridge to the west, its green flanks striped vertically with brilliant pink gullies. Mark explained that they were loaded with fireweed. I knew this fuchsia-colored flower from Wyoming; it was the trusty survivor, the plant that took root in ashes where forest fires had raged. Here in Alaska, fireweed evidently rooted itself in places scarred by avalanches.

Where tundra once flourished the resilient flower lived on. The gaudy pink stripes on the mountain slopes looked fake—like a photo tinted with too much color.

As the glacier steepened, the snowpack hardened. Walking required more effort, and I spotted a large, gaping crevasse off to our side. Mark chose to walk wide around it, but it was too close to ignore. The opening yawned, wide and dark. We'd left it behind, but as I followed Mark up a gentle rise I paused to look at the crevasse one more time.

I wouldn't want to fall into that one.

I mumbled those words to myself, and they've echoed in my mind for decades.

"Mark," I called. "I might need the rope soon."

That's how close I was to making a good decision. But my intuition was overcome with a youthful certainty that I'd never slip and fall. Not on a day like this one. Not me.

Mark paused at a level spot, took off his pack, and pulled out the rope. I took one careful step and then another. It would only take six or eight more to reach him, but doubt landed on my shoulder like a small bird. It fluttered for my attention—just for an instant—long enough for me to take the ice ax that I'd been using like a walking stick and throw its blade into the ice ahead of me. I figured an additional point of contact couldn't hurt.

The problem was that the pitch wasn't particularly vertical. I had to lean—actually hunch forward—to use the ax for balance. The front points of my crampons slipped free, and I began sliding. Then I somersaulted backward and slithered on the ice I'd just traveled. Thirty feet in a flash that I recall now in slow motion. First the beginning of the slide. Then a spin of unwanted motion. Surrender to a back somersault and a knock on the head.

More sliding, into air.

Down.

Into the cool, dark crevasse.

Mark must have stiffened watching me fall. He must have stopped breathing. The stillness at my disappearance surely stunned him. Mark the experienced climber. Mark the leader of the Alaska Rescue Group. Mark whose girlfriend had just disappeared into a huge crevasse on Byron Glacier. Unroped.

A wet ice wall, inches from my face. Water dripping. Then the sound of my own voice.

"I'm fine, just fine," I shouted, while noticing a bloody tooth, root and all, in the palm of a hand. It took a moment to realize it was my own.

"Well, I guess I lost a tooth," I said.

I was upright, stuck between two ice walls. Wedged in time, certain that everything was okay, except I had no idea what "everything" was. I did sense the importance of finding my way back—to reclaim my chronology.

Who was I, and where? Where did I come from? I had to start from the beginning. My memory was like a necklace that had broken, and I had to put its beads, one at a time, back on the string.

My name . . . Debbie. Debbie Clarke. I grew up in Connecticut, in the red house with white trim on top of the hill. Mom and Dad. College. Then Wyoming and a trip to Alaska. Mark and the expedition. Today: one more climb.

The gaping crevasse. We were just about to rope up.

"Debbie can you hear me?" A voice called—it was either Mark or Nick.

"Yes," I answered.

Then a rope dangled inches from my eyes. I couldn't figure out why it was there. Soon someone appeared alongside me. Mark tells me it was Nick, but I can't remember that part. All I recall is someone tying me to a rope, then pushing and prodding to free me from the wet grasp of ice walls. Then the sensation of being pulled upward along a slippery slab—and a voice coaching me to use my crampons. Finally I was pulled out of the crevasse, into brilliant sunshine that made me squint. Mark and Nick and Jill looked concerned; they told me to lie on a bunch of parkas.

"I'm fine," I told them.

"We know, we know," they said, while insisting that I lie down. Their smiles encouraged me, and together we talked each other into the reassurance that I was okay. They pointed out the perfect Z-pulley anchored in the ice. After a short while, they gave me permission to sit.

I stood.

We must have lingered for a while, but soon Mark and I roped up and he led me off the glacier. Then I followed him along the brushy path back to the car.

That walk was uneventful. I felt pretty good, never went into shock or even shivered. At one point I passed a hiker, who grimaced. When we reached the truck I took a quick look in the driver's mirror. My swollen forehead and nose, along with my mangled mouth, weren't exactly pretty, but my broken face didn't bother me. I'd made a big mistake by assuming I wouldn't fall into that crevasse. I'd seen it and decided to continue unroped.

Mark drove me straight to the Anchorage hospital, where I called Mom and Dad. They were eating dinner at the CM Ranch in Wyoming, where they were spending the summer. I remember Mom's response when I casually asked for the number on my insurance card.

"What have you done, and whatever is wrong?" she asked. She knew there must be a significant story.

I told her that I needed a stitch or two in my mouth because I had slipped into a hole when walking in the mountains. Not wanting to lie, I'd worked hard to come up with that description. It would have been painful to admit the truth: I'd made a near-fatal error.

It turned out that I lost more than a tooth and some pride on Byron Peak that day. I fractured my jaw, as well as my nose and two ribs. I also suffered a mild concussion. The doctors gave me a lecture about the hazards of the Alaska wilderness; they sent me home under the condition that Mark would wake me up every two hours.

Back in his condo, we set the alarm for midnight and agreed he would reset it at each waking. But I didn't want Mark to worry. Resolved to take charge, I slept lightly, and woke him five minutes before each designated hour to assure him I was fine. Nothing could rob us of the day's promise. We had to move on.

Three weeks after my fall, Mark and I set out to climb Mount Rainier. After the initial eight-hour hike, the pain in my ribs dulled my ambition. Then the following summer, when we hiked up a small mountain outside of Anchorage, I balked near the summit. There was a steep and exposed gully to cross.

Mark stood on its far side urging me on. "Just stand on your feet," he told me. "Take three simple steps. You can do it."

His words rang true, but I couldn't move—not on my own. Mark threw me a rope and reeled me to him, then quieted my trembling body.

"What's wrong with me?" I asked.

He paused before offering an honest answer: "You've lost your grace in the mountains." The truth hurt, but not as much as my terror.

Then Mark added, "You'll get it back—in time."

It might require many decades to reclaim my daring attitude climbing, but Mark and I needed little time to make a different decisive move. Exactly five months after the crevasse fall, we married in a hillside ceremony in the Talkeetna Mountains.

The January day was warm—maybe forty degrees—when my father and I walked along a snowy aisle lined by seventy friends who gathered outside the Hatcher Pass Lodge. Donning ski clothes and a new Norwegian sweater, I carried a bouquet of gardenias and roses. Instead of the long-imagined organ music in my Connecticut Episcopal church, the processional was delivered by my Austrian ski coach, Stefan, who stood on top of a nearby snowbank playing his ten-foot-long wooden alpenhorn. Its earthy call rang across the majestic alpine valley, echoing the ageless tenor of commitment.

Dad gave my arm a tight squeeze when he stepped aside to stand with my mother. Surrounded by both families and many close friends, Mark and I held hands and exchanged the traditional promises. Then we read passages written by climbers about the wisdom granted to those who go into the mountains, and the humility gifted from inevitable falls. The ceremony ended when Mark gave me a kiss and one of his ballroom dips. Then Stefan played his flügelhorn, and we all moved indoors for a hearty celebration.

Training run

6

Balance

In the dimming light of evening we cruise over rolling forested hills. Our recent getaway from the Manley checkpoint was orderly. Unlike our chaotic exit from Nenana, we left on our own terms and right on schedule, at 6:45 PM. At last we're running in ideal temperatures; it's cool, maybe zero. Lead dogs Taiga and Lil' Su set a perky trotting tempo we've practiced for hundreds of miles.

"Good girls," I say.

Only a few weeks ago I wondered if Taiga would make the team. She's always been happy to run in harness, but she's never overexerted herself. A longtime favorite of the family, Taiga has spent as much time on the couch as she has in the dog yard. When I discovered she liked to run up front, I hoped she could be a useful Iditarod player. Now she keeps pace with hard-driving Lil' Su.

What Taiga lacks in ambition, Lil' Su has tenfold. Bred by a competitive sprint musher, her original name was Krill. She and her siblings, Coral and Kelp, comprised the ocean-themed litter. I picked her out at eight months old. She was the spunkiest of the three: the black

45

girl with tan trim and bright blue eyes who leapt highest at the sight of her harness. Her breeders suggested I take her out for a test run, and that I could even try her in lead. She sped around the course like she'd been running up front for a long lifetime. I hastily wrote a check. Lil' Su has run lead ever since, winning more than a few racing titles with Hannah.

Now as the dogs click along the winding trail, condensation from their warm breath billows above the gang line. It's mesmerizing to watch them move through the dimming light, but I catch myself: nothing about marathon dogsledding around the clock is second nature. During the next five hundred miles, the turning of the day will become a welcome ritual, to run into the dawn an inspiring feat. But right now I'm going through mental lists, double-checking that everything is in place.

A quick touch to my right leg pocket confirms that my knife and Leatherman are where they should be in my snowsuit, and that two emergency granola bars are tucked into my right chest pocket. Matches, encased in a waterproof sack, are stowed in my left leg pocket. Two head lamps with extra batteries and backup lights are in the top of the sled bag, exactly where they should be. And a small emergency light is strapped onto my left sleeve. Head lamps have a tendency to burn out at the worst times. Long ago I decided there could never be too many spares.

Hopeful that I'm prepared for the night, I shrug my shoulders. Because of my heavily laden suit, the place between my shoulder blades burns. I'm thinking that it's better for me to be cramped up than the dogs when my mind trips on a different concern: we haven't passed a trail marker in a long time.

These wooden laths, painted orange on top and tagged with reflective tape, are easy to see in daylight or darkness. Every year five thousand markers are set on the trail to Nome. That sounds like a lot, but the number doesn't matter if you don't watch for them. Now, because I've been second-guessing my organizational skills, we might have veered off trail. It's no simple task, to turn a big dog team around and retrace our steps. Images of dogs in tangles, lines in knots, ornery exchanges, and a runaway team rush to mind. I need to face the possibility that we've missed a turn.

My handlebar watch peers at me like a giant eye: 7:45 PM. I decide to keep going in this direction until 8:00 PM. Those fifteen minutes last forever, but sure enough, an eventual flicker in the beam of my head lamp calms my fears. We're on course after all.

"Woohoo, it's all good," I tell them. At the sound of my voice Lil' Su turns and lends me a glance that lasts four or five strides. It's like she's saying, of course we're on track—she has known that all along.

We've been under way for several hours when Taiga and Lil' Su scamper up a steep windblown rise. As my sled crests the top I realize we're pitching down a drop-off that ends in a boulder-strewn creek bed. Within seconds a few dogs slip on the ice, and the team tangles in the boulders. I don't want to run into them, so I throw my sled on its side.

Don't let go.

Quickly they straighten themselves out and clamor to move on. It's not easy to right my heavy sled, particularly on the slick surface. I've managed to wrestle it halfway up when the dogs lurch forward. Gravity wins, and I'm down again, dragging.

Don't let go.

Momentum builds, and my knee cracks into something hard. The pain sucks my breath away.

Don't let go.

Finally there's a stump frozen in place, perfect to hook to and stop. My rambunctious huskies have no choice but to wait while I dust myself off and try to stand. I can't bend my knee, but somehow I manage. Grunting like a weightlifter, I wrestle my sled upright, pull the hook, and we're off, up that rise and down another. Eventually the trail levels, and Lil' Su looks back at me as if to make sure I'm still on the runners.

My knee throbs. When I touch it I'm relieved that the kneecap feels tight—it doesn't move from side to side.

God, it hurts.

I take off my gloves and manage to unzip my pants leg at the boot so I can slip my bare hand up my shin. There's no blood, another promising sign. Enough worry about serious injury. I need to watch where we're going.

We roll over a few small hills before reaching a windswept bluff. Trees are scarce here, and the few we pass are short and scrubby. Pieces of driftwood litter the trail's edge, reminding me of woods near the seashore. The darkening sky is particularly wide.

I've just turned on my head lamp when we pass a clump of markers and enter a flat, dark expanse. In the beam of my lamp, left and right, there's only black ice. Straight ahead is a perfectly white line of snow, punctuated in regular intervals with a trail lath. We must be on ten-mile-long Fish Lake.

Apparently the route was marked by snow machines—what we Alaskans call snowmobiles—when the lake was covered with snow. Wind must have later scoured the surface clean, everywhere except the packed and marked trail. As my mind clamors for an explanation, the dogs act spooked. Spot's hackles form a ridge on his back. Piney and Teton's ears flatten. Nervous Roulette looks back at me for assurance, and Strider slinks like she's afraid. I can't blame them. Gone are all landmarks such as rocky creek bottoms or hills to climb, nighttime silhouettes of mountains, or corners in the trail that surprise.

In this landscape of ice, there are no trees to tie off to and no easy way to stop. I loosen my ax from its straps. To chop a hole in the ice would be my only chance to set a hook. Satisfied with that adjustment, I'm calmed to see that Lil' Su and Taiga are willing to go. Even though their necks are unusually high and their ears erect, they trot steadily along the precise white line, lending courage to the dogs behind them. Every twenty-five yards when we pass a marker the beam of my head lamp picks up the flicker from five or six or more. They beckon like lights on a night runway.

It takes more than an hour to cross Fish Lake. With each mile, Lil' Su drives with more purpose; Taiga runs with ease. The cadence of dogs panting mingles with the click of their paw steps. My heartbeat softens, and my knee feels better. The watch on my handlebar no longer matters, and any interest in looking at the crumpled race schedule in my pocket slips away with the shore.

I don't notice the landscape's detail at first. I only see the dogs. Lil' Su charging and Kanga motoring in swing behind her. Spot's tall ears and Teton's worried glance. When they settle I look skyward to the stars and slivered moon—that's when I notice the northern lights. The green and blue filmy sheets glowing, falling, then folding and shimmering across the vast heavenly expanse. The lights sweep and swish and then fade away, only to reappear tinged in pink. Tethered only to one another, the dogs and I glide beneath the pulsing aurora. As we near the far shore, I yearn for Mark and the kids, wishing we could share this passage.

I'm walking up the steps of a log building in the Tanana checkpoint when I realize my left knee won't bend. The pain is dull, not too bad, but my leg is so stiff, I can't just *walk* up the stairs. So I hobble, one step at a time. Then I wrestle the heavy door open and limp into a warm, crowded room thick with rank air.

This log house is Tanana's Community Center, the official space designated for mushers to eat and nap. Our arrival in this tiny village means that my team and I have reached the Yukon River. We're three days and 250 miles into the race. So far I might have slept a total of six hours. My hands are swollen, my shoulders tight, and my leg stiff, but none of that matters because Taiga, Lil' Su, Kanga, and the rest are running strong. I'm giddy with a sense of accomplishment, but this is not the time to celebrate. I need to sleep.

It takes a while for me to make sense of this indoor space. Mushers are sprawled on the floor, sleeping. Snores rattle the musty air. Wet socks and jackets are draped on metal folding chairs, and coolers of meat thaw in the corner. It smells like sweat, wood smoke, and dirty socks—and the musky scent of wet dog.

Mushers aren't the only people in this cramped place. Race volunteers and other onlookers stand in clusters, whispering and sipping hot drinks. I recognize a neighbor from Denali; she nods at me with a smile. She's flying along the Iditarod trail, following her husband and daughter, who are both running the race. An NPR reporter who just interviewed me outside sits in a corner and scribbles in his notebook. I hope he got my story right. I want Mark and the kids to hear about our spectacular night run and know our dogs are thriving.

My groggy thoughts shift from one topic to the next, but the wise voice in my head insists that I get off my feet.

Go to sleep, Debbie.

It's critical to stay sharp for the long 120-mile run to Ruby. But before leaving in six hours, I need to organize and restock my sled. I should have done that before coming inside, but after I'd fed and massaged the dogs, my drop bags were more than I could handle.

The fact is that my drop bags—woven sacks sent to each checkpoint with restock supplies—are stuffed with too many choices. Why did I pack two kinds of kibble? And a short harness? Options of hot and cold meals? There's frozen lasagna that might have spoiled; I need to pack more of that disgusting freeze-dried beef stroganoff instead. There are booties and batteries and foot ointment, not to mention three different colors of sled-runner plastic. Without knowing the weather forecast, it's impossible to choose the best plastic.

During the course of this race I'll come to loathe my drop bags. Right now I'm flummoxed by the simplest choices, but I do know that sleep is pivotal. So I search for a place in the warm room to call my own. There's a metal chair, and it's empty. It makes a loud noise when I sit down.

My first chore is to take off my boots. This is no simple proposition. These arctic boots have "closed cell" liners made for mountaineers. They act like a dry suit, keeping my feet warm in subzero temperatures, even if they get wet. As long as I change into dry socks every day, they're perfect; but getting them on and off usually requires two people. Where is Mark when I need him? I point my toes as best I can, then use my right foot to push on the heel of my left boot to lever it. Of course my stiff knee objects, and I try not to kick the musher sleeping at my feet. It's a clumsy, painstaking process, but eventually I free my feet and pull off my socks to dry. I bundle my damp parka into the shape of a pillow and lower myself to the floor.

You would think I could sleep, but shivers zip down my back. This is all irritating because I've been warm outside for three days. But I just ate and am now in a state of chilled metabolic exhaustion. I have to sleep, or I'll doze off on the runners or start hallucinating—none of that is good. I need to relax, to count something like dogs or sheep or trail markers. Or think back to a day at home with Mark and the kids. I roll onto my back, but bright light stabs my eyes, so I grab a neck gaiter and lay it over my face. My stomach grumbles stroganoff. Maybe the calories will kick in quickly so the shivers will stop.

My mind jumps back to my sled: I should have restocked it already. We'll have to camp once or maybe twice on the way to Ruby, so there's a lot I need to remember to take along. Like extra dog food, and enough straw in case we stop twice. I can't forget three complete sets of booties rather than the usual two. Or that Lil' Su didn't eat well when we got here, so she gets extra lamb sausage before leaving. The runner plastic needs changing. I have to take my allergy pills, so I can sleep on straw next to Juliet when we camp. The head lamp that went out last night needs new batteries.

Don't forget.

My lips sting, and I reach into my pocket for lip balm. Then remember it's in my handlebar bag. There is no way I'm walking outside to get it. I roll onto my side, somewhere near sleep, and the dogs are surging onto the lake. We're moving through eerie darkness. Then floating in moonlight.

Dogs are yapping and screaming. I can't figure out where I am. I sit upright, look at a wall, and reel to the side, then lurch to my feet. It sounds like there's a dogfight, and it might be bad. But I can't stand. The walls spin, and I'm down on all fours trying to find my balance. Pain shoots through my left knee. The barking goes on, and I try to focus on something, anything. I've had vertigo on and off for a lifetime, and I know that if I can just focus on something—like that balled-up sock on the floor—maybe the spinning will stop. This time it's not so easy. I lean against the wall and struggle to pull on my boots, but my stomach lurches and I might get sick right here in this stuffy room with mushers sleeping and villagers watching. I remind myself that we're in Tanana, and my dogs might be in a brawl. I need to get outside quickly.

"You okay, Debbie?" a musher asks. He leans against the wall eating something. "You have vertigo, don't you?"

I nod yes and remember that Todd is a doctor. It consoles me that he recognizes my symptoms. The worst part about vertigo is fearing that it's not simply an inner ear condition. The anxiety that it might be something serious is not productive when you're an Iditarod rookie wondering if your dogs are engaged in a blood-drawing dogfight.

Nausea wells and my panic rises. I have to get out of this room. I weave out the door and hang onto the rail while lurching down the steps. My leg is so stiff, it might as well be wooden.

My huskies are sleeping—they're not the ones sparring. Sweet Teton lifts her head and watches me as I vomit my stroganoff into a snow-bank. Children giggle and scrunch up their faces. One says, "Yuck," and there's nothing I can do to show them my prettier self. I stand still for a moment, and the nausea subsides. Then I gather my nerve and walk—actually weave—in a zigzag to my sled, where I sit down and gulp the fresh air.

After an extended thirteen-hour stay in Tanana, I'm finally ready to leave. I feel better after resting on a couch for an hour in a back room and taking some motion sickness medicine. I've iced my knee. The swelling is down, and my leg actually bends. Although leaning over to bootie each dog makes me dizzy, I get the job done. There's no point in waiting around.

At 9:00 PM when I pull the snow hook and say, "Hike," the dogs leap to their feet. With the minus-fifteen-degree temperature soothing my seasick head, we speed into the night—away from the concerned officials, the musty room, and the children who smirked when I threw up in the snow. By the time we're under way, my head feels almost clear, my balance a little more steady. The sled bulges with extra provisions, and a half bale of straw is strapped on top. I don't think I've left anything behind.

We camp twice on the way to Ruby, once in the deep chill of night and again in the heat of the afternoon. It's close to 10:00 PM the following evening when the village lights come into view.

"Checkpoint, I see a checkpoint!" I call to the dogs.

Keno—he's taking his turn in lead alongside Kanga—begins his tall prance at my announcement, and the others perk up. Already trail-savvy, they know that the word *checkpoint* means warm beds of straw, a hot meal, shoulder massages, and attention from admiring children. They speed up, but we're all soon disappointed. The distant lights of Ruby elude us for another two hours.

Finally, near midnight, we climb up the steep bank to the village. Under the bright streetlights, we're welcomed by friendly locals and led to a parking place nestled alongside a red clapboard church with a short white steeple. It's been the longest single run of my mushing life, but at last we've arrived at a destination. We stop, and a volunteer holds out my leaders while I set the hooks. When I step off the runners, I can walk in a pretty straight line.

Debbie skijoring with Charlotte and Salt, winter 1990

7

The White Dog

In 1989, a decade after Mark and I met, our family lived near the end of a cul-de-sac in a new Anchorage subdivision named Spring Forest. Our four-bedroom home had gray siding and a steep cedar-shingled roof. Its red front door opened to a vaulted entryway complete with a circular staircase; beyond was a kitchen with maple cupboards the color of honey.

Hannah and Andy were five and seven at the time. They lived for exploring the woods behind our house and swinging high in the hammock stretched between spruce trees out front. Andy obsessed over everything mechanical—he spent hours in the garage taking apart lawn mowers, video cameras, or the old broken TV that he snatched from the pile for the dump. Hannah tap-danced on the hearth, slept in her pink tutu, and made every attempt to win games of Go Fish.

Mark and I enjoyed our shared purpose as parents. There was so much good in our busy lives that even a mid-pregnancy miscarriage at the start of the year hadn't thrown us far off course. With a survival instinct lodged deep in the bedrock of my New England genes, I'd shaken off my sorrow. By summer I was pregnant again. At twenty-three weeks Mark and I celebrated by telling Andy and Hannah they could count on a new brother or sister—that the death of one baby would soon lead to the life of another.

Hannah went with me to my next doctor's appointment. She played with her pink plastic pony while the midwife, Veronica, moved the scanning wand over my swollen belly. I'd come to cherish that wand of reassurance that monthly emitted a swishing heartbeat that echoed my own. This time the circling Doppler picked up my pulse— and a sea of static. Veronica placed her warm hand on my belly and tried again. Crackling. Empty noise. Like a radio when you can't find a station.

I turned my head, looked to the side at a rack of *Parenting* magazines. Then to the bulletin board filled with snapshots of babies with blue cords attached. First breaths. Euphoric parents posing alongside their midwife and swaddled newborns.

I inhaled, then swallowed rising pain. I prayed that time could hold off the words I'd heard before.

"I'm sorry, Debbie." Then she wiped the goo off my belly. "I just can't find a heartbeat. You need to go have a sonogram. You don't know how much I hope it proves me wrong." The wet line of a tear marked her face.

A few hours later Veronica's suspicion was confirmed. I was admitted to the hospital, one more time, to deliver my lifeless child. The memory of the earlier loss compounded this one. The labor and delivery ward, with newborns wailing their first cries. That child and this one, lifeless in a smear of blood. Once again, tests and theories were "inconclusive." For the second time in one year there were no answers—only the incomprehensible fact that our family would not number five.

Autumn that year morphed quickly into winter. The rivers seized up and froze, and soon the mountains donned a white shroud of snow. I'd always been a winter person, loved the rush of skis and sleds, downhill pitches into fresh, cool air. Not that year. When the night sky returned, I refused to look at the stars.

My mother, widowed several years earlier after forty-five years of marriage, took note of my grief. During one of our daily phone calls, she served up some tough New England advice.

"Debbie, you simply have to move on. These things happen. You've got so much going well in your life—be happy." She begged me not to put myself through another pregnancy.

My mother's wisdom was indisputable. Five years before I was born she'd lost a baby boy, who lived less than one week. Mom always called things the way she saw them, and for that I was grateful, but this time I was numb to her voice.

Well-meaning friends tried to offer support. "You have Andy and Hannah," one told me. "Two healthy kids. These babies must not have been right."

As if one human could ever substitute for another. To make matters worse, at my postpartum visit—the one when the doctor admires the week-old newborn and the office staff poses for those photos on the bulletin board—my obstetrician suggested that God must have other plans.

In an effort to flee from ceaseless chatter, I sought silent, empty places. Otherwise I'd bump up against unbearable noise, like the crying of infants. A sensation familiar to nursing mothers, the sound triggered the production of my milk, and my baby was gone. I ached for the life that only I had known. Songs on the radio about love of any sort reduced me to tears. I dreaded going to the grocery store, where a voice on the intercom announced sale prices on Pampers and a checkout clerk asked when my baby would come.

When the kids were at school, I stayed home. Even the view out the living room window had changed. Those shining peaks that Mark and I had scaled in summer and skied in the winter looked brittle, wind-scoured, and cold. For the first time in thirty-four years I spun a dark cocoon.

Soon after Christmas that year, our friend Bernie Willis called and announced that he and his wife, Jeannette, were coming to our house with a gift. We'd gotten to know them the winter before, when Hannah came home from preschool one day and announced that her friend Jani had sled dogs—and her dad was running Iditarod. Sure enough, her report proved true. Our family watched Bernie take off on Iditarod; he and Jeannette took us on sled rides after the race ended. Now came Bernie's voice on the phone, insisting that they would cheer me up.

I was in no mood for a present. No one would talk me out of my misery. But Bernie was determined: they wanted to give us a dog. Salt, he said, deserved a special retirement. He'd always been one of their favorites, and at age seven, Salt wouldn't run Iditarod again. Bernie insisted he would be a perfect addition to our household.

"Debbie, he'll be great pulling you on skis," Bernie promised. "You two can go as far as you want." He told me that he'd leave Salt with us for a week, and if we weren't getting along at the end of that time, he'd take him back. "You'd better get ready. We're coming right over."

When I hung up and told Mark what was about to happen, he chuckled and went back to reading his book. Andy and Hannah squealed with delight and raced up the staircase. I sat alone on the couch, vow-ing not to let the Willises or their old husky inside our door. No dog would ever replace what I'd lost. That much I knew.

As I sat on that couch dreading the ring of the doorbell, images of my past came back in a whisper. I'd grown up with working dogs—traipsing through autumn leaves following Dad and our Lab Pokey while she bounded ahead, trying to flush a pheasant. Years later I'd ventured on my first solo winter camping trip in Wyoming with a Weimaraner named Gus. Together, Gus and I shared an eight-hour ski and a minus-twenty-degree night in a tent perched in a high alpine valley. Together we witnessed the sunrise over the Bighorn Mountains and drank warm water melted from snow. These dog memories represented personal treasures, albeit from easier times.

My mom was visiting for Christmas at the time. She'd overheard our conversation and couldn't resist commenting that the last thing we needed was an old crippled husky.

"What is wrong with him?" she asked. "Why, I bet he isn't even housebroken!"

Her challenge prompted my swift defense. I told her that of course he was housebroken—having no reason to believe he'd ever spent a moment indoors. Mark raised his eyebrows and smiled.

Ten minutes later there was a knock on the door. Within seconds all three generations of our family met in the entryway to watch the old husky walk inside. After only a few steps the regal white dog with upright ears that tilted in a curve posed on our oriental carpet, cocked his head, and looked us over. Then he shook, from the tip of his nose to the end of his graceful tail. Wet snow dusted Andy and Hannah's charmed faces. Salt wagged his tail, apparently feeling quite at home. Then he trotted to our Christmas tree, circled it, and lifted his leg. For the first time in weeks, I laughed, and so did my mother. The white dog moved in.

During his first weeks with us, Salt rarely slept. Consumed with curiosity about his new surroundings, he had little interest in curling up on a dog bed next to the brick fireplace. Instead, he spent hours stalking our yellow cat named Meow and watching Goldie the goldfish swim circles in the bowl atop the kitchen counter. The rest of the time he followed me around the house, his wide eyes pinned on whatever I was doing. When I roasted a turkey, he quaked with desire. When I watered the plants, he cocked his head, anticipating his fair share. Salt offered me quiet, inquisitive companionship. He steadied my world.

One morning while cleaning the freezer, Salt tried to help. I offered him an ice cube, which he readily swallowed, but still he wouldn't pull his face out of the freezer. When he nosed a container of ice cream, I decided to offer him a taste. He licked the spoon clean, wagged his tail, and in no time at all he finished the pint. Later I learned he'd eaten frozen butter cubes during Iditarod. Vanilla Häagen-Dazs was the best thing he'd tasted since.

So began my training of Salt—or it might be more accurate to say that he trained me. Salt loved to ride in the car but had no interest in being a backseat passenger. He demanded to sit in the front so he could see where we were going. No matter how far we traveled, he sat beside me, often crammed next to a passenger. There was no negotiating. With his nose pressed against the windshield, Salt helped me drive.

I knew that sled dog leaders embrace pressure and thrive on guiding the team through difficult stretches of trail. So it came as no surprise when the weather was bad and the windshield wipers swept back and forth that Salt embraced the navigational challenge. One cold night when we were returning home from the grocery store, my defroster failed. Accelerating up a slippery hill, I scrunched forward, scraping the frosted windshield with a credit card. Salt bit at the glass so he, too, could see the road.

I came to expect entertainment when Salt accompanied me on daily routines. Nothing, however, prepared me for our first skijoring excursion. It was February that season when my spirits had finally healed enough that I wanted to get back onto my skis, and after all, Salt needed to run. One afternoon, when Andy and Hannah were in school, I dusted off my old climbing harness and pulled it on over an even older ski suit. Everything was tight over my hips and midsection, still flabby from the pregnancy. At least my gloves, boots, and woolen hat still fit.

As soon as I grabbed his harness, Salt ran laps around our yard. When I opened the car door, he hurtled into his seat. With skis, poles, and an old climbing rope stowed in the back, we headed several miles up icy roads to nearby Chugach State Park.

After parking at the trailhead, I rolled down my frosted window to get a better view. Salt bolted right out. I yelled at him, imagining that he might run down the trail and never return. There was no need for alarm. Salt trotted to a cluster of spruce, left his mark, and returned, looking expectantly for his harness. He stood still while I slipped it over his head and waited patiently as I put on my skis and carefully connected the rope from his harness to mine. Once we were clipped to either end of the eight-foot rope, Salt raised his nose to the sky and howled. Then he lowered his head and charged down the trail.

Somehow I survived the initial yank, and my old competitive ski legs lent me a short-lived sense of control. We sped along a wooded trail for nearly a mile and then came to a treeless open area with a ninety-degree turn. I was familiar with this corner that ushered us into a wide-open alpine valley. That day it was wind-scoured, covered with polished ice and rocks. Salt glanced back at me, seeking direction.

I gave him an emphatic "Whoa!"

The panic in my voice only encouraged Salt to speed up. He was likely wondering about going "gee" or "haw," but I had no familiarity with those directions. He tucked his athletic Iditarod legs under him and shifted into high gear. He bolted to the right; my skis caught on the rocks, and I fell over hard. We careened down the icy hill, me on my belly and Salt in an all-out lope. Eventually, a snowdrift slowed us to a stop. Shaking from the effort, I called Salt to my side. He slobbered my face with licks, and I responded with laughter. Interpreting my good humor with encouragement, Salt darted ahead and lunged to continue. I managed to stand and, with leg muscles burning, stayed upright as we sped several miles along a relatively smooth trail. We continued for an hour before my determined effort at a snowplow convinced him to stop. Then we completed an awkward 180-degree turn and retraced our route.

Craggy peaks cast shadows across the valley, and there was an invigorating breeze at our backs. Summits that Mark and I had climbed—O'Malley, Flattop, and Ptarmigan—cradled us as we slipped along the trail beneath their gullies. The sky turned to pale shades of purple and pink. Eventually the midafternoon moon rose over snow-laden mountains to the east.

"Good boy, Salt," I whispered.

He responded with a strong steady pace and zipped around the sharp turn at the top of the icy hill. Then together we sped through the scrubby forest. This time I noticed the stunted trees and the branches laden with new snow, the tracks of a moose that shadowed the trail, and the squiggly pattern left by a creature much smaller. I inhaled the scent of spruce carried on the cooling air and savored the prospect of the upcoming turn. As daylight gave in to inevitable darkness, the white dog took me home.

Hannah greeting Juliet on race day

8

River Miles

After sleeping five luxurious hours in Ruby, I wake to a cool, clear-sky day, perfect for mushing. I've just finished feeding the dogs when a villager trudges to my side.

"Your dogs look good; they're eating well," he says. "Trail upriver's good—all the way to Kaltag."

In winter the Yukon serves as a snow machine highway, linking villages. This man with local knowledge lends me confidence. To travel a functional route for the next several hundred miles means I might have a chance to shake off my vertigo and work the dogs into a steady run-rest tempo.

Other mushers do not share my positive outlook about running the river. Those eating breakfast inside the Ruby Community Center are tired and grumpy. They have nothing good to say about the 2003 re-route. One tells me that the two hundred Yukon miles on the traditional Iditarod route are more than he can stand.

"You have no idea how monotonous this damn river can be," he says, shaking his head. "You watch. They have us on one river or another for almost seven hundred miles this year. There'll be plenty of trouble."

Another agrees, using words like *brutal* and *ugly* to describe winds that can pick up for weeks at a time. Jim Gallea, a fellow musher who's raced with Andy and Hannah, gives me a smile and tells me to ignore all this negative talk.

"Take your time and watch your dogs," he says. "You know what matters."

Jim's words encourage. He reminds me that this course of extended river miles plays to my strengths in dog care. The normal Iditarod route passes through three landscapes: first the mountains, then the Yukon, and finally the Bering Sea coast. The variety of terrain and its weather defines the traditional trail's charm as well as its challenges, for dogs and their mushers.

On this unprecedented reroute, the mountain crossing has been replaced with 300 river miles, and the customary 160 Yukon miles have been more than doubled. I'm relieved to have been spared the treacherous snow-bare Happy River Steps and the Dalzell Gorge. The prospect of that crossing had haunted me all season. Now I look forward to keeping my dogs motivated and strong during extended river travel.

In the weeks that follow, some of the gloomy predictions will come true. Teams will struggle with the monotony of the 2003 "Iditariver." Seasoned lead dogs will sour, and so will their mushers. Veterans and rookies alike will be baffled by their inability to push ahead. In the end nearly one-third of the field will drop out of the race. More than a few will blame the river for burning out their huskies.

I don't foresee any of that when signing out of Ruby that morning. Instead, I'm looking forward to a perfect day of leader training. It's a little risky, but even though Sydney has never led before, I decide to pair her with playful Juliet up front. After I clip them together, they eagerly charge down the icy lane, take a sharp right turn, and descend a steep bluff to the river. The trail levels, the line tightens, and my tiny leaders settle into a spunky trot.

Juliet and Sydney run like puppies. They play on the fly, nosing each other and teasing with frisky nips. They easily influence the others, and it doesn't take long for Piney and Teton to mimic their game. Sleek little Strider prances; Taiga's tail puffs up. Even normally reserved Roulette nibbles at Spot, who motors along. The whole gang is acting like excited kindergartners heading out on a long-anticipated field trip. I'm one lucky teacher along for the ride.

We've been moving for an hour or so when everyone starts sniffing the ground—then they pick up the pace like they're chasing. Ever since leaving Tanana, I've noticed ski tracks on the trail. Usually they're covered with paw prints, but this morning they're fresh, like we might be closing in on the skier. When we round a bend, Juliet and Sydney raise their necks and charge. Spot and a few others woof as we pull alongside a fellow traveler.

The skier is tall and lean, with a European accent, a tan, leathered face, and a cracked-lip smile. I later find out that he's an Italian skier participating in the Iditarod Trail Invitational Race. He's far along on his journey, hauling a sled loaded with gear. Everything about him makes me feel lazy, just riding the sled runners behind my playful dogs.

"Good morning," I say, adding something about how nice it is to see him after following his tracks for so long. Before he can respond, Juliet vaults high into the air, then loops behind Sydney, tying her into a knot. I walk to the front of the gang line and untangle them. The skier points at my little gray bundle of energy and asks for her name.

"That's Juliet," I tell him. "She has a new nickname: Mouse of the Yukon."

Just then Sydney pounces at Juliet, instigating more mischief. As I try to keep everyone calm, I explain that this is Sydney's first time running lead. I regale the skier with details about my two thirty-pound leaders: how they romp together on summer hikes and insist on riding together in one "box" in the dog truck.

"They've always been best buddies," I say. "Just look at them now in lead!"

The skier smiles and nods. Then I laugh at myself and apologize for subjecting him to so much gushing. I want to ask him about his adventure, where he's heading and how long he's been under way, when Zeppy snarls at Nacho and Taiga begins to sing. They're all very entertaining, but this is, after all, a dog race.

I wish the skier well, and we zip down the trail. I turn and watch him follow, wondering how lonely he must feel to be traveling solo—without dogs.

Juliet and Sydney guide us all the way to Galena that day. When we arrive in early evening, I declare that we're staying for our mandatory twenty-four-hour layover. This is required of all mushers—to stop for a full day somewhere on the way to Nome. The long rest is a welcome chance to regroup. It's fun to dole out double beds of straw and offer the dogs extra kibble for dinner. To walk into the checkpoint and be treated to a homemade meal feels luxurious. There's even a mattress to sleep on, and running water for washing.

The benefits during our "twenty-four" are many, but so are the distractions. A race official warns me about dangerous snowless miles on the river near Anvik. A fellow rookie shares his feelings of homesickness and tells me he's considering scratching. The race manager talks on the radio in a heated exchange: something about double-checking that a rough section of trail is safe.

I call my family several times from Galena. When I ring Andy at college I can tell he is startled. Hannah's voice has a nervous edge, as though she's worried about saying something wrong. Compared with our children, Mark sounds uncharacteristically jolly. I know he is just trying to support me, but his tone dislodges the composure I'm trying to maintain. Maybe it's because our traveling rhythm has been interrupted, or that I have heard too many human voices, but as our twenty-four-hour stay in Galena comes to an end, my confidence wanes. I do what I should have done sooner: I go outside to rest on my sled, alongside my dogs.

My huskies are unfazed by checkpoint banter or words from home. They revel in the extended siesta. Having indulged in several huge meals, they relax in the warm sunshine. Kanga and Lil' Su stretch out in contentment. Nacho snores. Taiga sits up, studying a team that has just arrived. Juliet and Sydney are concerned only with one another. Curled together in a heap of straw, they lick each other's face clean. When they doze, Juliet drapes her head on Sydney's shoulder. At one point Piney tries to nuzzle in, and the normally calm Sydney bares her teeth. Three is a crowd for my proud new leader. She does not hesitate to tell Piney where to go.

When at last our long stop is over and I've strapped booties on all their rested paws, the team barks and howls. They're all wound up again, like they were in Nenana. Their crazed outlook worries me—we have many miles to go—but I don't let my fears slow us down.

It's around 8:00 PM and dark when I pull the hook and tell leaders Sydney and Lil' Su "Okay." They ricochet into a hairpin turn that descends to the river. Just when I think we might make it without incident there's a miserable *pop,* and my head lamp goes out. I lose my balance and tip over, but the dogs don't miss a beat. With noses to the trail, they bound into the darkness. Eventually I manage to right my sled and find a spare light.

The dogs run well that night to Nulato, but the miles are not carefree. We've been under way a few hours when Sydney develops a hitch in her gait. At first I try not to notice, but it's undeniable: she's favoring her left front leg. I stop the team and run up and take off her booties, hoping she's reacting to an uncomfortable fit. Still, it's there: a tiny tick. I try everything, first switching her to the other side of the gang line and then running her in a different kind of harness—anything to make her more comfortable. Every time we stop, she rolls in the snow, then lunges to get going. She shows no hint of pain.

When we pull into Nulato, I'm eager to ask the vet to diagnose Sydney's problem. After carefully manipulating her joints, Caroline confirms my suspicion that it's her pectoral muscle. The soreness is mild but unlikely to improve with massage. She recalls Sydney from an earlier checkpoint and tells me something I already know.

"It might not be worth it to push a young dog," she says. We both understand the importance of being conservative. Caroline continues, "Feed them dinner and think about it. Come find me if you want to drop her."

There is no debate. It's best to call Sydney's first Iditarod a success right here and send her home. I try to convince myself that she won't be disappointed, that the deep, rising sadness is mine. Not wanting to postpone the inevitable, I unhook my pretty red leader from the line and lead her to the dropped-dog area. A muscular black husky is alone on a line, bellowing. His team has just pulled out. Holding my breath, I sign a piece of paper, hand Sydney to a volunteer, and walk away. I can't say good-bye.

When I return to the team, determined to shake off my sorrow, Juliet lies alone in her double nest. Her ears are flat, her nose on the ground. When I sit next to her, she doesn't lift her head. She wants Sydney, not me.

By the time we reach Grayling, I've done the math. We've been on the Yukon for five and a half days, and we've completed six out of ten runs on the river. Something like four hundred Yukon miles are behind us; nearly two hundred remain. In hindsight, the endless river hours and miles merge into one extended effort; we follow a line worn in the snow, usually straight, passing a marker every so often. The dogs trot along for ten miles. Then I stop them for a treat. When I say, "Hike," they trot some more.

We travel for no more than seven hours at a stretch and try to rest an equal amount. We spend extra time in the comfort of checkpoints, where I massage each friend, dole out two big meals, then find my way inside for my own food and rest. Every bend of the river leads to another; daytime slips into a darkness that eventually lightens into dawn. Sometimes when temperatures rise to forty degrees, we rest through the afternoon. On those days we run all night, in the cool, invigorating darkness that the dogs love.

As the marathon miles accumulate, my dog team and I enter a topography of shifting time and space. One afternoon I'm certain that we're running uphill, and then I remember that for God's sake, we're mushing on a river. My mind wanders from one random thought to another. I might spend ten minutes wondering what day it is. Then that mystery folds into another.

What is a day?

Somewhere on the river I decide that an Iditarod day is defined by the upcoming checkpoint. Instead of Monday and Tuesday, it's Ruby and Nulato. Then Kaltag. Eagle Island. Now Grayling. This is Iditarod's measure of time.

When we pull out of Grayling I'm fully alert. This is the run downriver to Anvik, where we'll turn around and retrace our steps upriver. These are the miles I was warned about back in Galena—images of treacherous black ice and a blustery wind have crouched in my mind ever since. I've made sure to leave in early afternoon so we can complete the down-and-back course in daylight. I'm glad to have Kanga run in single lead. She's one of the few who enjoys taking charge up there on her own. Juliet and Taiga are behind her in swing, offering support. I'm counting on Kanga's pride and her veteran wisdom to keep us safe.

During the first eight miles out of Grayling the trail hugs the right shoreline; it's snow-covered and smooth. Then, as predicted, a sweeping turn shoots us into a wind-scoured, hostile landscape. The change is dramatic: the river ice is smooth and black, interrupted with jagged fissures and hairline cracks, sometimes patterned like a spiderweb. Scattered across the wide expanse are logjams and a few boulders, locked in ice. It's a spooky black landscape, void of winter's white. I might be able to find beauty in its dark palette, except all I can do is hang on.

I clutch my handlebars and brace myself against a gust of wind that slaps us from the side. The sled skitters sideways, and the dogs are frightened and look for decent footing. Of course there isn't any, so it's up to me and Kanga to figure out where to go—to stay clear of driftwood snags, broken trees, and boulders lodged on the Yukon's hard surface.

Kanga is drawn to this dangerous game. For an hour or two she and I share an intense conversation. "Gee, girl, gee over. Okay. Straight ahead, now haw. Good girl, thank you," I tell her. Whenever I speak, she responds.

Kanga steers us clear of one obstacle after another, but the wind is relentless. Inevitably it catches my sled like a sail. Then I careen off course, bending my knees in anticipation of the hard slap when the runner catches on a jagged crack that makes my sled slam over. Usually there's some consolation in leaving a difficult section of trail behind, but that thinking doesn't apply here; when we reach Anvik we will have to do this all over again.

Kanga senses my angst. She looks at me over her shoulder frequently and alters our course to compensate for a dangerous swing of my sled. Once I crash hard and the dogs get tangled in driftwood. Kanga turns toward me for a few steps, as if to evaluate my trouble. Then she moves to her side, lining out the team along a different angle, which sets us free.

I'm relieved when we make it to Anvik; we check in and out in a hurry. I change a few booties while volunteers stand on my brake and toss each dog a hunk of lamb fat. I give Kanga two helpings; she wags her tail and gobbles the treat, then tugs on the line, urging me to keep going. Juliet rolls and woofs in swing behind her. It's like they've known all along that we would turn here and retrace our steps upriver.

Northbound the wind poses more of a challenge. Confident that Kanga knows the way back to Grayling, I ignore the trail markers and direct her onto thin stripes of snow near the middle of the river where there's less debris. It's a tricky request to ask a leader to leave an established trail, but Kanga revels in the challenge. At the sound of "Gee" she raises her head, then bounds to the right. We continue on untracked ice for hours. Again and again, Kanga crosses the shortest distance of black ice, from the relative safety of one snowy drift to the next. Then she turns, looking to me for the next instruction. Together, in a fierce swirling gale, we react to the wind and forge on.

What began as a terrifying trip on black ice turns into a performance of grace. No longer worried about crashing, I engage with Kanga in an intimate and rare conversation. The dog's drive to please is unmistakable; her resolve to chart a new and better course is an honor to share.

Kanga guides us safely back to Grayling. With the precision of a master, she leads us past one perilous snag and then another. When we leave the black ice behind, I stop the team and run up to thank her for the finest miles I will ever share with a leader. I don't yet know that these are some of her last leading miles.

One more river run is permanently etched in my memory: our final run on the Yukon, from Eagle Island to Kaltag. After a rest of eight hours at Eagle Island, the dogs are eager to go. At the sound of "Hike!" they leap to their feet. Energized by the dimming light of sunset, leaders Kanga and Lil' Su guide the team off beds of straw and onto the trail. All ten leave the Eagle Island checkpoint in a prance, their heads high.

"Way to go, Debbie!" a checkpoint volunteer cheers. With this kind of attitude on the line, she knows our seventy-mile run to Kaltag will be strong.

One mile down the trail, as always, I stop the team and give all the dogs a chance to relieve themselves. Kanga looks distracted, maybe sleepy or bummed. So I take her out of lead and put her back, where she greets her new running partner, Spot, with a bitchy little nip. Meanwhile Lil' Su impatiently lunges. Nacho and Roulette pause to pee, and sisters Piney and Teton rub their faces on my legs while I adjust the Velcro on their coats. Farther back on the line, Taiga rolls playfully on her back, wanting a belly rub. Never mind that she's a tough Iditarod dog—she is still a princess.

Four hours pass and so do forty miles. The temperature is perfect for mushing, something like ten degrees; we're moving at an impressive ten-mile-per-hour pace. When darkness deepens, the sky brightens with a canopy of stars. I've grown accustomed to turning off my head lamp to witness the night. Now in the dim moonlight, the dogs seem to float, black on white. The sound of their breathing blends with mine.

The clear sky is the last thing I expect that evening. The ham radio operator at Eagle Island told me gale-force winds were in the forecast, so I hustled to leave the checkpoint in order to beat the storm. We've been under way for five hours when I hear the first eerie whistle. I won't want to stop and snack in the midst of a storm, so I toss each dog a hunk of beaver. While they gobble the frozen treat, I replace a few booties that have holes in them and make sure each dog coat is securely fastened.

I might be an Iditarod rookie, but I know about being prepared. It's critical to make sure that the dogs and I are fed, hydrated, and clothed in order to move forward. When I reach Spot to check his booties, he looks at me and cocks his head.

I answer his inquisitive gaze by whispering his favorite word: "Sing!"

In response he raises his nose to the Yukon sky and sounds the first note. The canine chorus joins in. So do I. A storm may be coming, but when my huskies and I are stopped on that wide river, our lungs fill with song. All is right in our world.

When our howl ends, insistent barking begins. Spot chews on the line and Lil' Su jumps in the air. This team is what veterans call "trail hardened." Nothing will faze them now. There's a light breeze, and I'm sure we'll beat the storm to Kaltag. I step back onto the runners and whisper, "Hike."

Then we zip upriver.

We're close to Kaltag—within ten miles—when the first snowflakes swirl. Quickly the sky folds around us. The dogs are all set, but I have to get myself in order. I reach for my goggles and then cinch up my sled bag. Then I tighten the strap of my head lamp, making sure to keep it clear from my hood and its wolverine ruff. A touch of my hand confirms that my spare head lamp is still in my arm pocket, and that my matches and emergency food, knife, and Leatherman are stowed in my suit.

The trail hugs the wooded left-hand shore, and a turn of the river delivers us into fierce whiteout conditions. Streaks of white pour into the beam of my head lamp. The swirling suggests vertigo, giving me that disoriented and woozy feeling. The wind stings, and I'm worried about keeping Lil' Su up front as a single leader. I've tried Juliet with her several times, but ever since Sydney's flown home, Juliet acts tentative in lead. This is no time to experiment, so I clip Kanga alongside Lil' Su. When I ask them to go, Kanga cowers; I put her back with Nacho. It's a lot of pressure on Lil' Su, but for now she's the best we've got.

"Good girl, Lil' Su, straight ahead," I say, encouraging her onward. She looks back at me before veering toward the bank, apparently seeking shelter beneath an overhanging tree.

"No, Lil' Su," I shout. "No, no. On by!" At the sound of my voice she takes a few steps forward.

I've heard of storms that you simply can't travel through, but to camp now is unthinkable. Yes, I could crawl into my sled bag, and the dogs could burrow into the shelter of the snow. We'd all survive, but these ground blizzards can linger for days, and Kaltag is near. We need to keep going.

When I run up the line and pull Lil' Su away from the bank, I'm alarmed to see the others dogs cower.

How quickly everything can change.

As I hustle back to the runners, I'm looking at dogs' faces that are all white, masked with snow. With urgency I call, "Hike!" This time Lil' Su lowers her head and drives into the storm.

An hour passes as we forge into a frigid wind tunnel. The temperature might be reasonable, around zero, but the wind accentuates the cold. I cover my nose with my neck gaiter, and my goggles fog up. To take them off would risk my eyes, so every few minutes I scrape ice from the lenses with the back of my arctic mittens. In some places the trail is scoured clean, and we gain momentum. At other places the dogs have to wallow through drifts three feet high. I try to help them by getting off the runners and pushing the sled.

My huskies trudge on, their noses to the ground following the scent of other teams who've been here before us. Every hundred yards or so, I'm comforted to pass a trail lath. Whenever Lil' Su reaches one, she searches for the next. Marker to marker. We move into the blizzard.

The wind isn't steady that night; gusts shift from one direction to another. I'm feeling disoriented, almost confused, when two bright lights appear to our side. At first I don't trust that they are lights, so I turn off my head lamp briefly to make certain they aren't just reflectors on markers. When they remain, I'm heartened.

Pleased to have company on the trail—probably two snow machines—I blink my head lamp repeatedly. I want to connect, maybe even team up, with these storm travelers. They come closer and I wave in gratitude. They cruise alongside us, never getting near enough for me to see the drivers, but lending us courage to go on.

For a long time we travel alongside the friendly beacons. My shoulders relax, and I sip hot chocolate through the straw of my thermos. The lights stay near but never move in front of us. Their presence is a comfort, and the dogs and I watch them. Once in a while Lil' Su surges ahead, like she's excited to have something to chase.

As quickly as the snow machiners appeared, they vanish. Power lines connect the lights, illuminating rooftop gables. Our companions are actually lights of Kaltag. It takes me a while to get over my humiliation; for an hour I've been waving to the village. Then I decide none of that matters. The lights gave me what I needed: escorts through the storm.

The dogs might have understood reality all along, but when they notice the rooftops of Kaltag, everyone accelerates into a lope. We've been on the trail for nine long hours when a gust laced with the scent of gasoline and woodsmoke ushers us up the ramp to the village.

It's around 5:00 AM when the team trots alongside a row of small buildings in Kaltag.

"Whoa." I call them to a stop.

There's no need to set my snow hook—the dogs know we're in a checkpoint and quickly lie down. Stumbling up the gang line, rummy with exhaustion, I wipe snow from each face and talk to each dog. Gratitude consumes me, but I can't linger. The best I can offer Lil' Su and the others is to find them a sheltered place where they can rest and I can cook them a well-deserved meal.

I walk to a building in hope that it's the Kaltag checkpoint. It seems odd that after our harrowing night there's no one to greet us. When I lean against the door it opens, and I'm encouraged to see stacks of drop bags. I shine my head lamp up a dark, narrow staircase and shout a raspy hello.

At first there's only snoring. Then a voice and some rustling. Finally a figure appears. She covers her eyes from the glare of my light and greets me.

"My God, Debbie. Is that you? I can't believe you ran through that weather. We didn't expect you tonight."

The New Zealand accent is unmistakable; Kirsten is a fine veterinarian who's flown across the globe to tend to Iditarod dog teams. Now she hurries down the stairs and wraps me in her arms. I'm thinking it must not feel very nice to hug my ice-glazed filthy self.

She congratulates me while putting on her parka and her boots. Then together we walk outside, where she leads us to a sheltered alley where the dogs can rest out of the wind. I pull my cooker pot out of the sled and stagger back to the building to get some water. When I return, Kirsten's checked over each dog.

"Debbie, they look wonderful!" she says.

Kirsten delivers confidence. Despite the wicked conditions, and my marathon exhaustion, my huskies ran with brilliance tonight. Now they look to me with weary eyes. While the water heats, I visit each one. Kanga moans with gratitude while I rub her shoulders, and Juliet leans against me with uncharacteristic surrender. Lil' Su's light-blue eyes draw me closer.

Despite my nagging allergies, I lie on the straw alongside her and rest my arm on her side. Feeling the rise and fall of her breathing, I'm certain that nothing inside me compares to her courage and her honest, steady heart.

Salt and his little protégé, Suds

9

Mentor and Friend

Salt had retired from Iditarod when he walked into our house, but he had everything to do with my eventual journey to Nome. From the moment we met, Salt showed me how a husky and a human could collaborate in adventure. We were inseparable traveling companions.

We skijored together in daytime when the kids were at school. One snowy night we snuck onto groomed Nordic ski trails and swept down steep turns by the light of my new head lamp. In summer we hiked valleys of lush green tundra. When berries ripened, Salt watched me pick; then he licked his fair share from my blue-stained hands.

To Salt I confided my deep maternal sorrow. In response he shared his devotion for the trail. The irresistible curve of his cream-colored ears framed a gaze impossible to ignore. Daily he insisted that we focus on the next best thing, and I could not turn him down.

I look back at our first year together as a season of mutual discovery. Salt had an uncanny ability to read my mood, and I did my best to interpret his desires. The scratch of his paw on my knee and his woof at the door insisted that the mountain air was waiting. If we ventured there together, we wouldn't miss out. We simply had to go.

It was in Salt's company that I came to accept Dad's unexpected early death. In the safety of his unconditional acceptance, I wrestled with the possibility that there would never be another child. With canine patience that never flagged, the old retired Iditarod dog drew me from grief's hold. As he did, I found my way back to Mark and Andy and Hannah—and to them Salt gave even more.

One year after joining our family, Salt and two nine-month-old sidekicks, Moxie and Morgan, had reordered our days. We'd sold our ski cabin south of Anchorage and re-landscaped our suburban backyard. Hannah had lost interest in swimming classes, and Andy ignored requests to join the Boy Scouts. During boring meetings at work, Mark designed doghouses and cedar-sided pens. I searched for a part-time job that would pay for the highest-quality dog food and lend me flexible hours so I could manage the fledgling Salty Dog Kennel.

I might have been Salt's original protégée, but Andy and Hannah were first in our family to try racing. Hannah could hardly see over the sled's handlebars when, at age six, she and Salt sped around the one-mile one-dog course. Andy was old enough for the three-mile two-dog event, which he entered with speedsters Moxie and Morgan.

Junior races were set up like the adult ones. Mushers and their teams took off in two-minute intervals. Little mushers had victory dreams for sure, but it wasn't only about competing. To venture onto the trail with a family mutt or two meant embarking on high adventure—completely on their own.

Hannah's one-dog escapades were never dull. Salt sang for every countdown and leapt into action to the sound of "Hike." He lived for a good chase, but whenever he caught up to a slower team, Salt stopped to investigate. If the competition was a pretty little female, he couldn't resist sniffing around. Hannah tired of Salt's extracurricular interests and eventually opted to try the more competitive Morgan. Named after a favorite second-grade teacher, the blue-eyed seventy-pound yearling had more ambition than sense—and no intention of staying on the short one-mile loop. Weekend after weekend, Morgan challenged volunteer trail guards by hurdling a snow fence, dumping Hannah in the process, and charging solo onto the longer, three-mile trail.

The one-doggers and their trusty canines charmed onlookers and parents, but it was the two-dog event that provided high-stress drama. Eight- to nine-year-old competitors took off behind pairs of dogs who, combined, far outweighed their mushers. Completing the three-mile course took the better part of twelve minutes. There were moose to avoid and a warm creek that flooded the trail, making conditions icy.

While families awaited the return of the two-doggers, sometimes the radio crackled and a trail guard announced that little Johnny's dogs were inbound without him, or that all ten teams were in a tangle waiting for a moose to get out of the way. Sometimes driverless sleds pulled by gleeful hounds skittered across the finish line; it felt like hours waiting for breathless little mushers to follow on foot.

In the end junior races always had happy endings. Those memories will long sustain me: Andy's hearty voice calling "Woohoo" to Morgan and Moxie as they galloped inbound. Salt cocking his head as Hannah handed him a finish line treat of turkey leftovers. Our elated children and their tail-wagging comrades rolling in the snow. Eyelashes and whiskers frosted from the cold.

In all seasons Salt served as master trainer for our huskies. He led post-meal songs and guided young puppies on summertime excursions in the woods behind our house. One day the kids and I leapt over a small creek, and Salt waded across at our side. Then Taiga, maybe three months old, started yelping, refusing to follow. She raced back and forth, looking for a narrow place to cross. Salt barked at her once, then splashed up to her as if to show her the way. When his stubborn student refused, he circled behind her and nosed her in. She had to comply.

As our dog team matured, Salt offered advanced water lessons. It all began one day when the kids went canoeing on a small lake where we camped on weekends. Salt leapt into the water behind them and swam in their wake. As they neared shore a few minutes later, our other six huskies jumped in. Mark and I stood in disbelief watching our children paddle the canoe in front of a buoyant white dog followed by several pairs of others, splashing and huffing along. Our huskies swam two by two, following their leader. Those swimming workouts would become a regular summertime highlight—for all of our dogs except Taiga. She raced along shore barking disapproval, making sure to keep her royal paws dry.

In February of 1993, when the children were eight and ten and our backyard dog team numbered six huskies, Mark came home with a State Parks map of the Nancy Lake Canoe Trail. We'd camped there in summer, paddling the chain of lakes while Salt swam alongside us. It seemed strange that Mark would plan our next canoe trip in early February, but he had something else in mind. We'd run our own dogs, along with a few borrowed from the Willises, ten miles to the remote cabin where we'd stay for spring break. We had five short weeks to get ready.

Mark took charge of gathering necessary equipment, while I focused on meals. Together we made lists and accumulated necessities such as an ice auger, a short-handled ax, and a pack saw. We sewed booties, bagged kibble, and talked our butcher into saving us fat scraps for the dogs. Andy and I met with Karin, our veterinarian, who helped us put together a canine first aid kit. The Willises loaned us a third sled, and Bernie showed Mark how make a tie-out cable so we could safely secure the team. Our children were full partners in the preparations. Andy proudly wore his own knife on his belt. Hannah served dinner to our growing team of huskies by the light of her pink head lamp.

When spring break arrived, one neighbor flew to Maui and the other took off for the smooth ski slopes in Aspen. Meanwhile our family and dog team drove on icy roads to the Nancy Lake canoe trails north of Anchorage. We must have been a spectacle: four people and Salt crammed into the small cab of our little pickup, ten huskies peering out of six "dog boxes" set over the truck bed, and two bales of straw and three dog sleds bulging with gear on the roof. Nothing could have made us happier.

The ten-mile trail to the James Lake cabin wound along twisting forested portages that linked a series of lakes. Mark was first on the trail that year, driving a five-dog team led by Salt and Moxie. Andy followed with three dogs and Hannah with two. Each sled was bulging with food and provisions for our weeklong wilderness stay. I followed with a heavy pack on my back, skijoring the unruly Morgan. He and I were to act as "trail sweeps," dusting off thrown mushers and picking up gear strewn on the trail.

We traveled in sight of one another, sweeping through elegant stands of birch and slipping through sunbeams that mottled the snow. Sometimes the shaded trail was ice-hard and rough. The trick was to hang on for the ride along the portages, then regroup while crossing the lakes on snow softened by the warming March sunshine.

It took almost two hours to reach our destination. The James Lake cabin was sixteen by twenty-four feet and sat high on a bluff overlooking the lake etched with a trail—and no other hint of civilization. The inside of the building was perfect; its airy space held everything needed for comfortable living. There were bunk beds for sleeping, a small table for cooking, and an old barrel stove. On the stove's rounded surface teetered a pot, which we constantly fed with snow to melt for drinking water. On each wall of the cabin were big windows that offered views of the wooded lake country around us. The largest overlooked the front porch and the dogs, nestled on their private beds of straw.

The front corner of the cabin housed a big square table lined with two wide benches. Everything happened at that table. We ate meals there, worked on a jigsaw puzzle, and studied maps. Skittles, KitKats, a Robert Service book, and a few candle lanterns sat on its wax-splattered surface.

During that first visit to James Lake we took turns mushing two at a time. Mark and Andy set off exploring for five long miles and dared to run over the steepest portages in the hills beyond the lake. They returned ruddy-cheeked and chatty, challenging Hannah and me to do the same. We headed in the opposite direction, intent on claiming our own fun.

There were trails to investigate and discoveries to enjoy: the playful squawk of the raven by day and the eerie hoot of an owl by night. The pop of lake ice cracking. We followed tracks of lynx and hare and quietly stalked a playful ermine who lived under the porch. Stories around the dinner table took on mythological proportions. We wrote truths in the logbook as well as a few lies. Tall tales were part of the fun.

To spend a week at James Lake was to engage with our dogs in navigating the winter landscape around us. No longer captive to the customary roles of "parent and child" required in town, we savored a deepening bond with our huskies—as well as one another. Beholden solely to the terms of the wildness in which we lingered, we were all children at James Lake. We shared curiosity about tracks in the snow and watched the woodpile hoping for an appearance of the resident ermine. All four of us howled with Salt and his chorus; then we listened for a response from the black moonless night. Mark treated our kids to his favorite mountaineering concoction: brandy peaches. Andy showed off by successfully running a four-dog team over a steep tree-lined portage that repeatedly dumped the rest of us on our sides.

For four years we went to James Lake in springtime. Every season we arrived with a few more huskies and explored longer trails. The milestones were many: the first twenty-mile run and then the first thirty. The first time the kids mushed alone in the dark.

Perhaps most memorable of all was the buns-of-steel contest, when the kids dared each other to run to the outhouse naked, recite a complete Robert Service poem, then roll in the snow. As Mark, Salt, and I sat in the cabin enjoying the warmth of the woodstove, we listened to breathless renditions of the final lines from "The Cremation of Sam McGee":

> There are strange things done in the midnight sun
> By the men who moil for gold;
> The Arctic trails have their secret tales
> That would make your blood run cold;
> The Northern Lights have seen queer sights,
> But the queerest they ever did see
> Was that night on the marge of Lake Lebarge
> I cremated Sam McGee.

Then came the sound of our huskies outside yapping as they watched their naked young musher flop in the snow before dashing inside.

On our last trip to James Lake in 1996, Salt had just turned sixteen. Because he could no longer keep pace with the team, he and Mark walked to the cabin while the rest of us mushed. Mark snowshoed and pulled a toboggan he'd made from native birch for the occasion. Salt trotted at his side, relinquishing his leadership role to elders Morgan and Moxie, and a young pup named Taiga.

By day and night that year Salt slept at the foot of my sleeping bag. He occasionally ventured onto the porch to oversee an incoming dog team, and he moved well when it came time to walk out with Mark to the truck. It turns out that Salt never returned to James Lake. Neither did we. Maybe it's fitting that the cabin on the bluff and the old white dog live together in memory—in a context that outlasts time.

Lil' Su

10

From the River to the Sea

The morning after we make it through the storm to Kaltag I'm standing in a doorway wanting to ask a volunteer where to find my drop bags. He's chatting on the phone and doesn't know I'm waiting.

"Oh man, wish I was with y'all. Must be some party." I imagine he's talking to someone in Nome, where champion Robert Sorlie has crossed the finish line after completing the course in nine short days. Iditarod's victory celebration is in full swing.

I'm only half listening when the volunteer says my name: "Moderow arrived during the night." He continues to explain that there are others on the trail behind me. "Evidently a few are thinking of scratching. I hope they all scratch. The sooner the better, if you ask me."

I hope they all scratch.

At first I can't move—as if something's exploded and I don't know where to run. Then I recoil and walk away before he sees me. Back to my dogs.

They snooze in the late morning sunshine. When I approach, Lil' Su raises her head. Then she stretches her legs behind her and burrows into the sun-soaked straw. Her thigh muscles flex and her black fur shines. Just to see her softens my outlook. I kneel beside her and rub her shoulder. It was here in Kaltag, three hundred miles ago—the first time we came through—that she stood up on three legs. Her triceps were cramped in a painful knot, and the vet showed me how to massage it out.

"If you do this after every single stop, she might get better, Debbie. Give it a try," Denny advised. I didn't really believe her, but during the long miles downriver and back, Lil' Su has healed so well that she runs without a hitch. Now she leans into me for her daily massage. As my fingers circle in her warm fur, my own shoulders loosen.

I hope they all scratch.

He has some nerve. The fact that Sorlie has won Iditarod when we have yet to reach the coast has no bearing on my thirteen-day schedule. We are right where we should be: less than three hundred miles from Nome. My sole purpose has always been to finish with a healthy and happy dog team. Those are my terms of success. I'm okay with a few more days on the trail.

That's what I tell myself, but the criticism echoes in my weary mind, accentuating a gloomy scene around us. There are rows of used straw littered with feces and uneaten snacks. Someone hasn't gotten the job done, cleaning up after teams take off. Shovels and rakes are strewn here and there, and a few shredded garbage bags are tangled at the base of a light pole. A gnawed-off beaver foot lies in the snow next to Lil' Su. Some old scraps of fat tempt Teton and Piney. I kick the debris away and sit on top of my sled.

It's hard to imagine this is the same Kaltag we passed through three days ago. We were heroes then; now the volunteer wants us to scratch. Just last night we pushed through a blizzard; today we rest in hot sunshine. I want to curl up on the straw with Juliet, Kanga, and Lil' Su, but I know better. There's no telling when we'd wake up. So I push through chores, restock my sled, and by mid-afternoon I ask the team to get back under way.

My dogs leave Kaltag in fits and starts. I'm expecting them to act invigorated after a ten-hour rest here, but they feel tentative and so do I. When I call encouragement to leaders Juliet and Lil' Su, I'm trying to rally myself. I wonder if Yukon storms deliver a delayed reaction.

The trek from Kaltag to Unalakleet follows a traditional overland route, long used to connect the river to the sea. Our journey along the ninety-mile portage is arduous; snow is scarce and ice-glazed sidehills make for difficult sled handling. I had hoped the dogs would perk up when we got back into the forest, but whenever my sled slithers sideways into a rocky creek bed and tips over, Lil' Su and Taiga voluntarily stop. While I work to right the sled, eleven pairs of dog eyes watch me. Nacho sits and so does Roulette. No one tugs on the line to go. When I ask them to continue they do, but their usual spunk is gone. Like they left their good cheer on the river.

For seven slow hours we slog onward. We move for a while and then we come to a glaciated slope. I tip over. The dogs stop and stare. Then the cycle repeats. Finally, in the early hours of morning, dog ears perk up and the team accelerates. A few minutes later we pull into an open area in front of Old Woman Cabin, the legendary resting place halfway between Kaltag and Unalakleet. Another team is bedded in straw here; their musher must be inside.

I welcome the break but am sorry to arrive in darkness. I know from reading Iditarod trail notes supplied to rookies that we're stopped in the shadow of Old Woman Mountain, whose slopes allegedly avalanched, taking the life of the old woman who called this area home. Now, as I melt snow for dog water, I realize we must have passed her original cabin, the one that houses her ghost. Mushers are advised to throw her a treat when going by; failure to appease her can jinx the coastal run ahead. Now, through a thin veil of exhaustion, I rally and ask her forgiveness.

If I'd seen your place, I would have tossed you my biggest chocolate chip cookie.

After feeding the team I go inside, where the other musher moans and tells me she's sleeping off the flu. In order to avoid getting sick, I forgo the warm sleeping quarters in favor of napping in my sled. With my sleeping bag pulled tight around my face and my hands on my chest, I finger a good-luck charm that hangs on a rawhide string around my neck. It's a fossilized walrus tooth, carved on both sides: one shows a face encircled with a ruff, the other is the profile of a walrus. I've worn it for more than a year with the Bering Sea coast in mind. I hope it delivers good fortune.

We leave Old Woman after several hours of rest and embark onto a well-trod forty-five-mile route to the sea. Here the trail leaves the forest and crosses a wide-open hillside covered in scrubby tundra. Perhaps it's the warm morning sunshine or maybe the monotonous terrain— for whatever reason the team does not move well. Creek trots alongside Nacho fast enough to keep up, but really, neither one of them is pulling. In lead, Lil' Su and Taiga chug slowly on.

Even my memories of those miles are sluggish. My eyes are so heavy with sleep that I try shutting one and then the other, in a misguided attempt to prevent nodding off. I do recall signposts, tripods with large numbers: 770 . . . 771 . . . 772. It takes me a while to realize these numbers represent miles of the Iditarod Trail. They could well encourage weary mushers to celebrate the distance already traveled, but to me they document our turtle's pace. I vow to ignore them, but the resolution is easier said than done. One tripod irritates me to the point that I close my eyes to avoid seeing it. Sometime later I wake up to the sight of my dogs snoozing on brown tundra—and we have yet to pass the damned sign.

Eventually the trail dips into the cool shade of the woods. The dogs' pace quickens, and soon we reach a bluff overlooking the sea. There's a wide expanse of ice, patterned with strands of silver water, and the smell of salt on still air. In an apparent mood swing, my huskies cruise along that hillside and scamper down to the Unalakleet River. Broken trail markers litter the icy surface, and it's impossible to know where to go. Lil' Su and Taiga sniff the patterns of brake marks, following the scent of others who have traveled here before us.

The possibility of losing the trail here is real, so I decide to put Kanga alongside Taiga in lead. She's been here before; I'm hoping she remembers the way to the checkpoint.

This time Kanga is willing. She and Taiga charge past weathered shacks and old boats on shore. The river widens, and the team accelerates over an eerie patch of turquoise ice. Within a short mile, when we round a gentle bend my leading pair lopes toward a group of people clustered around a few bales of straw. As we pull in, an elderly Alaska Native gentleman with smiling eyes greets us.

"Nice leaders," he says. "I haven't seen a team this strong in a couple of days. You'll make it to Nome no problem."

"Thank you," I reply, trying to mean it. I'm proud that the dogs ran into the checkpoint so well, but that's not exactly how they've moved for the last ninety miles. Maybe Kanga made the difference. It might be her time—again.

After an eight-hour rest in Unalakleet, we get back onto the trail. It's early evening, the sky's glowing orange, and Lil' Su's in single lead. Soon after leaving the checkpoint, we're navigating a series of sloughs on the Unalakleet River. The first is covered with a skim of snow, and then we come to another. This slough is a mirror: one hundred yards of polished ice fit for a figure skater.

"Straight ahead!" I call.

The dogs take ten careful steps, then a few more. I wish I hadn't bootied them—they're having trouble gripping the ice. Piney's front legs splay, and she slips. Teton freezes in a wide-legged stance, and the others pull her along. Juliet slows and picks up her feet in an awkward prance. Nacho's ears flatten. Lil' Su looks back.

"Straight, Lil' Su, straight ahead!" I plead, thinking that if we can just get halfway across, they'll scramble toward the security of tall exposed grasses on shore. Lil' Su hears me and tries to move, but Nacho sits and so does Roulette. Before I draw another breath, they all stop. Ten dogs wearing crimson coats sit on a mirror of ice beneath a sky the color of salmon. The reflection teases with beauty, but the reality stings.

Focus, Debbie. Focus.

I need to make a good decision. My huskies can't move, and if I try to slither up the line and lead them forward, there's a good chance they will tangle. So I decide to take off their boots. Maybe better traction will repair their lost confidence. This is no easy task, to get from my sled to the dogs. I slip and fall but manage to get the job done. When I ask them to go, they don't budge.

Daylight is fading when I begin to unhook each husky. I'm confident they won't run away; once they're loose, surely they'll run to the security of shore. Then I can push the sled to the grassy edge of the slough.

One by one I set each dog free. Nacho claws his way to the grass. Creek and Lil' Su go together, shoulder to shoulder, as if they are still on the line. When they reach decent footing they play like young pups, romping and rolling on their backs like they do on summertime hikes. Roulette sees things differently: she curls up in an immovable ball. And Spot and Juliet choose the nearest security. They jump on top of my sled and sit down as if seated on a throne.

The next move is mine. I wrap the gang line around my waist and pull the sled, with its royal passengers, toward the shore. When I call the dogs, most of them come. Not Roulette. She remains on the ice in her rebellious little knot, so I shuffle back to her and coax her onto her feet. It takes at least twenty minutes to re-bootie the gang and put them back on the line. It's dark when we're back under way, heading up the Blueberry Hills.

I've long heard of these hills. The name conjures up images of rolling tundra covered with berries in August. Several Alaskan artists have painted pastoral renditions of Iditarod teams climbing gentle terrain on a snow-covered trail lined by willows dusted with frost. But this reality is different.

For three hours I fight to keep the sled upright on sidehills of dirt and ice; progress is slow and my performance clumsy. The team is willing but my psyche is frayed. I'm worried about my huskies—they just aren't acting right. Then my imagination flares. I see buildings where there aren't any, snags on cliff edges that threaten free falls into darkness. I tip over on a mild turn that shouldn't have knocked me off kilter—while fixating on Juliet's gait. She's favoring her right front leg.

After several hours wrestling one phantom or another, we reach the crest of the hills and an unexpected reward: we're gliding on a trail of soft fresh snow. Before I can adjust to this mythical sensation, the dogs accelerate into a sweeping downhill turn. Sometime during that glorious half-mile descent, a clutch of ptarmigan takes flight alongside us. They're in full winter plumage, white like doves.

When the trail levels, I stop the team and throw everyone a congratulatory snack—and notice the distant lights of Shaktoolik. Elated by the sight, we take off again, speeding down one more pitch. One last descent delivers us onto the beach, smack into a wall of frigid, raging wind.

It's like we've moved from one world to another. I throw in the snow hooks and run up the line, cinching down dog jackets and tightening the strings on my hood. I'm alert, no longer weary. The wind requires my full attention. When I holler the command to go, Lil' Su's ready. For the second time in two days, she lowers her head and trudges into a gale whose punch is something we've never known before.

We push on for several hours, me calling encouragement and my dogs trudging forward. Most of the time it's impossible to know if we're on or off trail; every once in a while we pass a reassuring brake mark on the wind-scoured ice. All I know is that we have to keep moving. And that Juliet's not pulling, but her gait looks okay. I'm fixating on whether or not to load her into the sled when suddenly a swirl of snow delivers us into the beam from a light post. Then we come to another.

Snowflakes spin and the air shrieks as we make our way along the icy village lane. Then a gust catches my sled from behind and pushes us all forward. Without warning the dogs veer to the side and stop next to a small building. At first I wonder what's happened. Then a gust settles, and I see a hooded figure shuffle out the door. Denny, my friend and vet, shouts a welcome to Shaktoolik.

Andy and Taiga

11

Childhood Dream

When Andy was in third grade he was asked to write a little book; it came as no surprise that he produced an illustrated volume called *Hike*. In it he described his adventures as the first kid musher to run the Iditarod.

Checkpoint by checkpoint, from Anchorage all the way to Nome, Andy traveled with his mighty two-dog team: Morgan and Moxie. He endured a series of challenges by coming up with resourceful solutions—like the time his handlebar broke.

"Luckily I had bubblegum along," he wrote, "or I wouldn't have been able to fix it." He was also glad to have stuffed his pockets with candy. When the moose charged his dog team, he tossed her a candy bar, successfully diverting her attention.

From the start of the race in town, through the treacherous terrain of the Alaska Range, and onward into the coastal blizzards, Andy and his huskies survived. Finally, they pulled into Nome in the middle of the night. It was only then that he realized that they had won the Iditarod.

"BANG!!!" wrote Andy. "Fireworks were going off! Microphones hanging off fishing poles were all around me! Even my teacher was there with my mom and dad. It was some party! . . . It was the happiest day of my life."

Ten years later, in 2001 when he was eighteen, Andy's childhood dream came true. During that season between high school and college he worked as a dog handler for Iditarod champion Martin Buser. In exchange for helping to care for and train Martin's 120 huskies, Andy earned the honor of running Buser's second string of dogs to Nome.

We were celebrating Hannah's sixteenth birthday when Andy left home to go live with the Busers. Her party was winding down when I noticed Andy standing at the door. Donning a bulging backpack and carrying a guitar under his arm, he motioned to me that he was ready to go.

I hadn't completely anticipated the gravity of this parting. In my mind, our son was temporarily moving an hour north of town to follow his Iditarod dream. So when I walked up to my seventeen-year-old son to give him a hug, I didn't recognize my own rising sadness.

Andy did. He looked to the side in discomfort.

"Bye, Mom," he said, and then added, "You know things won't ever be the same around here—so don't pretend they will." With his tongue stuck in his cheek, he turned and walked away. Mark fled to the dog yard to complete chores, while I sliced myself a second serving of Hannah's chocolate mousse cake.

One year later Andy ran the Iditarod. The winter of 2001 had been unseasonably dry, and our son had pushed through nearly impossible training conditions to help prepare two teams at Buser's kennel. At age eighteen Andy might have been young, but he had years of experience. He'd lived for our dogs since early childhood and had completed the 150-mile Junior Iditarod four times. He'd won several Humanitarian

Awards for exemplary dog care and had just spent a full season apprenticing for a master. By the time he left the starting line, Andy knew far more about distance mushing than anyone else in our family. His youthful vigor and always happy energy was well suited for the challenging snowless conditions. He and his dogs rocked the Iditarod Trail.

Andy's race gifted us with a series of good surprises. Familiar with my capacity to worry, Andy promised to call home often—and he did. The phone would ring, and Mark, Hannah, and I took turns listening to his breathless upbeat reports. There were stories about leaders Calvin and Bill, and predictions that eventually he might need a little more sleep. When we read in newspapers about mushers twice his age getting battered on rocky descents or beaten down during a Yukon windstorm, Andy reported that the challenges had been no big deal. He entertained us with chatter about camping with famous mushers and singing with his team in a squall. Evidently one night in the high mountains when he turned off his head lamp, it looked like his dogs were floating in starlight.

Andy did get spooked when he arrived in Shaktoolik. He didn't call from that coastal checkpoint, but from race updates we knew he stayed there for an uncharacteristically long time. When he phoned from Koyuk the next day, he explained that Shaktoolik had been a "scary place." He described an "evil wind" and told us that he postponed leaving but in the end had no choice.

"It's all good now, Mom," he reassured me. And it was.

Running into white

12

Sea Ice

My alarm rings at 5:00 AM. I rub my crusted eyes, sit up, and look around the room. Folding chairs are draped with wet jackets and pants; the usual clutter of socks and boots are drying near heaters. There's one plastic table stacked high with food and another with an orange canteen marked *Tang*. A series of crayon drawings by local children hang on the wall. One reads, *You can do it Debbie Moderow*. Beneath the caption are a pink stick-figure musher and a blue dog with bunny ears. The message encourages, but my head pounds. I lie back down and close my stinging eyes.

I'm listening to the wind when another musher starts talking. "What can you tell me about this next run?" Kelly asks Rhodi, the race judge.

"Follow the markers and not the tripods," she answers, explaining that the sea ice never froze this winter, and that the tripods lead to open water. Race judges are the checkpoints' go-to people. They watch out for the well-being of all. "Don't be fooled by the sled tracks," Rhodi continues. "Aliy went the wrong way, got to open leads, and had to turn around. Stick with the markers and you'll be fine."

Not again.

I'm thinking we've already skirted open water on this race. Shouldn't once be enough? No wonder Andy thought this place was spooky.

Kelly mutters for a while and then poses another question: "You got a forecast?"

"Yeah, they're calling for winds—up to sixty knots. But it's not supposed to die down for the next three days, so you might as well go. No point in waiting around." Rhodi describes a lone hill called Island Point eighteen miles out, where there's a shelter cabin that could come in handy if the winds increase. After the cabin, the trail takes a turn to the east. "From then on, the wind should be at your back," she says.

Kelly asks more questions and the answers are detailed. Rhodi talks about the notorious thirty-mile sea crossing to Koyuk, confirming what Andy has told me: that the miles on the ice will feel endless, especially since you can see the lights of Koyuk for hours.

"Don't let them fool you," she says. "You'll get there."

From the confines of my sleeping bag I try to rally, but last night's run in the gale haunts me. *What were we doing out there? Alone?*

There's no good answer—I know that. I busy myself by flexing one foot and then the other, which triggers a miserable cramp in my hamstring. I grab the back of my thigh and try not to scream. Eventually the pain fades, but now my swollen fingers throb. The vet in Kaltag did her best to fill cuticle splits with superglue—she told me heart surgeons use the product regularly. I hope someone here can patch them.

Concentrate, Debbie. Come up with a plan, the voice in my head reminds me. *Forget the fingers. Find the drop bags. I sent a dry shirt here. I'll change, eat a big meal, then wake the dogs. They need a good meal and water. Maybe we should cut rest here, in order to leave with Kelly. There might be safety in numbers.*

My thoughts shift to the dogs, hunkered down in beds of straw on the other side of this flimsy wall. In my mind I see their crimson jackets plastered with snow. Frost on their noses. Lil' Su's heavy blue eyes.

I hope they feel better than I do.

Then I remember Juliet. Denny confirmed that I should leave her here; it's the right thing to do. Now thinking of leaving our tiny cheerleader behind brings on a wave of emotion. But I remind myself that Juliet hates wind even more than the cold. She might be happier at home. With Sydney.

We'll all be there together soon.

At 8:00 AM we're ready to go. I've eaten a three-egg omelet and fed the dogs a double meal. I'm donning every piece of available clothing: over the usual three layers and my snowsuit, I've added insulated pants and another down parka. Then an oversized white anorak designed for arctic weather. My sled bag is cinched tight, the dog coats are securely fastened, and booties are on.

I motion to Kelly that she should go first. When she claps her hands and says, "Hike," her huskies stand. A few stretch and some others look stiff. They move at a slow walk around the corner of the building and are gone.

Rhodi helps me rearrange my dogs, clipping Piney into Juliet's empty place next to Teton.

"Fly safely home," I tell Juliet out loud, like she's my good-luck ladybug. She's already been taken from the line and out of sight, but I whisper again, "Fly safely home."

Then to the others I call, "Let's go." They shake off sleep and stand. A few kind villagers guide us around the building and over an icy snowbank. They shout farewell, and I hold on tight as the team scrambles down a bluff to what looks like a beach. A gust swirls around us, but the dogs trudge on. They move past several markers to an enormous orange fabric fence positioned to protect the village from drifting snow. As we approach, it flaps an ominous rattle. When we round it, we face directly into a fierce and frigid gale.

Kanga's in single lead. She led so well that last mile into Unalakleet, I'm confident she is up to this challenge. Now she slows, sniffs the ground, and stops. Quickly I run to her side.

"What's up, girl, do you need company? I'll put Lil' Su up. Good girls!" I praise them, clipping Lil' Su at Kanga's side. After patting them both, I hustle to my sled assuming the problem is solved. When I pull the hook and call, "Hike," no one budges. Lil' Su and Kanga stand still. Roulette and Strider sit down.

At first I wonder what I've missed. The wind is blowing, but at least it's daytime. This is nothing compared with last night. Not wanting to ask too much of Lil' Su, I take her out of lead and put Taiga up with Kanga. They move a few steps, until Kanga sits down and Taiga rolls in the snow.

This time I choose Creek. "Good girl," I tell her, putting her in lead for the first time in the race. "This is your big chance!" It takes a minute for me to reorder the whole team. Lil' Su and Creek are buddies, so I put them in lead together.

Satisfied that everyone should be pleased with an exciting new arrangement, I cry, "Let's go!"

And they do.

They trot for several minutes. I'm thinking that of course every-thing is fine when Nacho stops to relieve himself—and everyone else decides he has a great idea. Spot and Zeppy lift their legs. A few girls squat, while Roulette and Kanga sit down.

"No!" I call, with heightened alarm. Again I rearrange everyone and plead, "Let's go!"

My dogs tune me out. With heads hanging, they look off to the side. When I wipe the frost from her muzzle, Kanga pulls away. Lil' Su pretends I'm not here.

After trying every possible combination, I position myself alongside Lil' Su in lead. When I ask the team to follow, she and I tug them to their feet. My huskies must be surprised to see me up front. At first they agree to move, but a jolt of momentum jerks the riderless sled, which nudges the wheel dogs in the butt. Insulted, wheel dogs Spot and Creek sit down, and so do the others.

The rejection is unbearable. I go back to being the musher.

Our game of charades continues for at least another hour. I hoot and holler encouragement, then talk sternly in hopes of winning some respect. I gesture with my arms, offer smiles and frowns. We move one half mile at a time. Then they balk, and I try something different.

Sometime during our struggle, a red plane with a yellow stripe swoops low overhead. I don't hear it approach; when it flies near, I wonder how long it's been there. The plane looks familiar, like the one flown by a friend who takes fans flight-seeing over the trail. It circles over us a few times and then leaves, only to reappear a half hour later. This time it flies quickly past, and I'm glad. It's devastating to consider how we must look from the air.

As much as I don't want to be that musher with her dog team, stopped in a great white expanse because the dogs refuse to move, the possibility that our race could be over doesn't yet occur to me. That sort of thing happens to greedy mushers who push too hard, not to me. Still, there's no getting around the fact that we have a real problem: eight hundred miles into Iditarod, my dogs no longer hear me. In an attempt to reconnect, I walk dog to dog to dog. One friend to the next.

Cleaning frost from Taiga and Lil' Su's faces, I tell them how far we've come, that there are fewer than 180 miles to Nome. When I pat Kanga and rub her shoulders, she stiffens like she doesn't want me to touch her. Teton's blond face looks more worried than sweet, so I stroke the soft hairs between her eyes.

"Good girl," I tell her. "We'll get there."

Piney is running solo in the middle of the line. She doesn't like wearing a coat, so she's pulled the Velcro belly band loose. When I tighten it up, she nuzzles her head against my jacket. At least there's some connection there.

Roulette and Nacho look sullen. Roulette won't even lift her head. "We'll take a double layover in Koyuk," I promise her.

Spot and Strider are in front of the sled in wheel. Strider's floppy ears droop more than usual, her stare is blank. Spot looks better; he's eyeing something off to the side. When I scritch his ears he responds with a single tail thump.

"Thanks, buddy," I say.

Interacting with my dogs one by one settles my panic, but a single tail wag doesn't add up to much. I ask them to go one more time, in a simple and upbeat tone, but I'm not surprised at the lack of response. So I walk to the front of the line and sit on the ice alongside my leaders. I consider one fact at a time.

It's not like we can stay here in the wind.

We have to go somewhere.

Maybe we should go back to Shaktoolik.

To be stopped with a dog team stuns me; to even think about reversing course on the Iditarod Trail represents an incomprehensible defeat. I have watched a few teams return to checkpoints during the race. When a rebellious string of huskies came back to Eagle Island after leaving, the checker opined that the musher was ruining his dogs. At the time I agreed: it can't be good to let them have their way. But if they won't run ahead, what's the option?

As my huskies doze, I know we need to do something. It doesn't take long for me to choose a peacemaking role. In hope of negotiating a new beginning from the comfort of a checkpoint, I take Lil' Su by the collar and walk the line into a 180-degree turn. I point my dog team back toward Shaktoolik.

This time when I step onto the runners and call, "Hike," the wind is at our backs and everything is different. Kanga's ears stand tall, and Spot lets out a woof. Roulette lunges. For the first time in two days, Strider wags her tail. When I pull the snow hook there's no need for a command—the animated team breaks into a happy-dance lope. With a spunky spring in their steps, my huskies charge back toward Shaktoolik.

We've been moving for only a few minutes when a snow machine with two riders appears. A villager is driving the checkpoint volunteer. They wave me to a stop and suggest that we reverse direction and follow them toward Koyuk, to the shelter cabin at Island Point.

"It's only about thirteen miles away," the volunteer says. "If your dogs will follow, we can lead you that far. Maybe they'll get moving, and you can run right past the cabin. You can always rest there if you need to."

Her well-meaning words confound me. At last the team is happy; we've shifted into a new plan. Still, I worry about letting the dogs have their way. When I begin to describe my dilemma, she cuts me off.

"Look, Debbie. You need to make a decision. We don't have all day." At the time I realize she's coaxing me to focus, but her words sting.

What does she know about my "day"?

For nearly two weeks I've slept maybe four hours each "day." We've traveled through eleven nights and "days," navigating whiteouts and black ice, persevering through Yukon River storms and one dark coastal gale. A gust screams and too many choices spin in my head. While I struggle to understand her plan, confidence in my own falters.

"Okay," I answer. "We'll try it."

It feels wrong when I take Lil' Su's collar in one hand and Taiga's in the other and walk them back into the wind. When I stretch out the line, they all sit down. Their ears are sideways flat, their noses pointed to the ground.

The snow machine pulls ahead, and my huskies stand. In an attempt to be open to every option, I decide to try Spot in lead. He's never agreed to run up front, but there's no denying he's the happiest dog on the team. When I clip him on the line next to Taiga, he noses her and wags his tail, but the sound of "Hike" doesn't register. He sniffs her butt, then swings back to visit with swing girls Piney and Teton.

With that experiment over, I put Lil' Su back up with Taiga and call the dogs to their feet. This time they move ahead in a resigned walk. I ride the runners shouting praise, while inhaling humiliating fumes of exhaust.

That we're moving at all should be encouraging, but at the time all I know is that we're following this Iron Dog because my huskies will not run on their own. They won't run for me, but they will chase a snow machine. It's like I am nothing to them. That's the worst of all.

Nearly an hour passes. The wind rages on, but that has become standard. My humor improves with each mile. We're moving at a decent slow trot when the cabin comes into view. I'm heartened at the opportunity to run past it, and I hope the dogs are also. The snow machine veers away; its riders wave me past.

"On by, on by! Good dogs, on by!" I shout.

The trail comes within a few feet of the tiny shack, and Taiga and Lil' Su accelerate.

"On by, on by!" It all feels so promising until they dart to the left. Mistaking the exposed grasses for beds of straw, Lil' Su and Taiga bolt to the lee of the building. They paw at the bedding and circle to lie down. I try everything to dissuade them.

"No, Taiga! No, Lil' Su!" I holler, pulling them back on course.

"Ready, ready? Hike!" I call. They bolt back to the cabin.

"No!" I repeat, and quickly reposition them on the trail.

"Stay, Lil' Su. Stay, Taiga. Bad girls. You stay."

I hustle to the runners, but before I utter a command, they're back at their new favorite place. Again I pull them into the wind. Pat and praise them, encourage and beg them to move on.

My huskies look away from me in defiance. The wind wails, and the walls of the cabin groan. Then I recall the words of an old musher: *You can't push a rope.*

My dogs get their way.

"Guess we'll be here for a while," I say to our escorts, and thank them for their trouble. Before they take off, I pose a question that's nagged for hours. "Was my family on that plane?" I ask.

"Yep, that was them," the volunteer responds. "They landed and told us you were stuck. They're taking it pretty well."

Her words steal my breath.

"Okay, we're outta here," she adds. "There should be a few more teams coming tonight. Maybe your dogs will follow. Good luck, Debbie."

As the drone of the snow machine fades, I busy myself with my huskies. After taking off booties, I wrap Piney's wrist and give Lil' Su a shoulder massage. I try to shake off my exhaustion and be alert to their signals. I'll collect snow and melt it for their next wet meal. I remind myself to eat and drink in order to be my best for them.

As the dogs and I settle into our familiar camping routine, the shock of their shutdown fades. We've stopped to rest on many trails and then moved along. This time should be no different.

"We'll figure it out," I tell them. "We have to."

Mark, Andy, and Debbie after Andy's
2001 Iditarod finish in 17th place

13

Legacy

The last time Andy called us during his Iditarod was from Koyuk. With 140 more miles to the finish, he recognized that he had a competitive chance to finish in the top half of the field. From that checkpoint forward, he focused on competing. Reports of our Iditarod son came to us in race updates and newspaper articles that described the amazing young rookie and his happy dogs cruising toward Nome.

From Anchorage all the way to the coast, Andy had been the happy-go-lucky youngster on the trail. Free from any competitive expectations, he had nothing in particular to prove. With youth on the runners and veteran dogs out front, Andy and his team thrived during miles of snow-bare conditions. Since his two-dogger days, impeccable dog care had always been Andy's specialty. For the first half of the race he stuck to a conservative schedule with ample rest. His team grew ever stronger.

By the time Andy and his huskies reached the final coastal checkpoints, they were on a roll. He surprised even himself by keeping company with a pack of well-known professional mushers. Then, in a quickening tempo, he passed one after another. When he realized he had a chance to finish in the top twenty, he cut a rest short and went for it. He and his spunky dogs motored on.

I'd never been to an Iditarod finish before when Mark, Hannah, and I flew to Nome to celebrate Andy's finish. As our plane began its gradual descent, I pressed my face against the ice-glazed window and tried to comprehend the treeless white landscape. If I hadn't been looking so hard, I would never have noticed the hint of motion beneath us. A dog team looked like a segment of thread lying on a sheet cake with vanilla frosting. It seemed inconceivable that this musher and huskies had traveled the country we'd just flown over. I knew I could be watching one of Iditarod's superheroes gliding toward victory, or possibly looking at our son. Then I eyed an open lead of water linking the ocean with shore. I wondered what it would be like to run a dog team so close to the sea, never imagining that one day I'd find out.

I hadn't heard the sound in years. The siren that went off in Nome whenever an Iditarod musher reached the outskirts of town was the duck-and-cover alarm that rang through my Connecticut elementary school during Cold War civil defense drills. In Nome that shrill wail signaled that a musher and dog team were on Front Street, minutes from the burled-arch finish line.

At the siren's call, everyone streamed out of bars, hotels, and houses to witness the team's moment of triumph. Nighttime finishes were particularly festive. Strings of Christmas lights crisscrossed over the finish line chute. Spectators could see the head lamp of the musher bobbing at the end of the street long before making out the silhouettes of the dogs. Daylight arrivals might have been less romantic but offered a better view of huskies running, the musher waving, and a jubilant crowd cheering them in.

We'd been in Nome for two days and witnessed sixteen mushers finish when the siren blared. The sky was bright blue, and the seventeenth-place musher coming down Front Street was our son. Just a few blocks from the finish, the team zipped along, looking like they'd been out on a frivolous ten-mile jaunt. As Andy and his dogs moved effortlessly toward us, I wanted them to pause, or at least slow down, so I could savor each step. First were the dogs, their heads high and tails floating behind. Then Andy. He rode the runners for a while, then jumped off to sprint alongside them—to be one with his huskies.

When Andy stopped his team under the arch, he was surrounded by officials and press wanting stories from the youngest musher in the 2001 field. He tried to politely hold off the questions, insisting that first he needed to snack and praise the real heroes. Encircled by an admiring crowd, he moved up the line to thank leaders Bill and Calvin. Then he walked toward his sled, speaking intimately to each dog. In the narrow shade of the arch, he shook hands with the race marshal and hugged Mark and Hannah. Grinning with something much more than pride, he pulled me into his strong arms.

"Mom, you have to do this," he said.

I knew, right then, that I would.

Teton bedded down on the trail

14

Shelter Cabin

My nine huskies sleep in the lee of the plywood shack. I sit on top of my sled and watch them, curled in tight nose-to-tail balls atop dead grasses that poke through the wind-scoured snow. They look almost content, snuggled two by two in their crimson jackets. Like resting here might be part of our plan.

But my dogs know better, and so do I. The truth of our trouble rushes at me, and I swivel in place, turning my back to the wind. The cabin door rattles, and for a moment the air quiets, like it's taking a breath. Then a new gust wails. Taiga startles awake at the crescendo. Lifting her soft red head, she squints and flattens her ears. She looks past me with empty amber eyes.

I follow her gaze to the barren landscape we've traveled. There's nothing but white. No trees, just an empty expanse with a faint line of a trail and a few wooden markers that vanish into the haze. This isn't any kind of haze I've seen before. It's different from the ice fog that settles in our valley at home in Denali on the coldest winter days. Or the August mist that curls in and around the gangly black spruce and eventually lifts to reveal sun-soaked mountains. This is an evil hood-wink haze. The air moves so steadily, it tricks the eye and appears still. Snow crystals race above ground, suspended in an incessant Bering Sea wind.

In one more effort to take charge, I stand and get moving. My hamstrings ache and my frost-nipped chin stings against my frozen neck gaiter, so I rotate it—which helps my chin, but now water drips down the back of my neck. I tighten the strings of my wolverine ruff and burrow into its dry warmth. Thank God for the wolverine. Maybe now I can think straight and come up with a plan.

Better to look ahead than behind. Look to Koyuk.

With self-imposed wisdom I stumble past the dogs, ten paces into the gale. It's not easy to see the outgoing trail—there's white ice and an occasional stripe of snow. A marker pitches toward ground, and a piece of driftwood lies at my feet. When I pick it up, its splintered surface sticks to my woolen gloves. I touch it with my tongue and, sure enough, taste salt, proof of the sea. It's nice to be certain of something.

This place is so locked in winter that I can't tell where the land ends and the ocean begins. This knob of a hill must be Island Point. From what the checker said, we're only thirty miles from Koyuk. To be stopped here is nothing but wrong.

Never mind, Debbie. Take care of yourself, so you can help them.

It's been hours since my breakfast in Shaktoolik, so I fumble in my pocket for a granola bar. It's frozen solid, and the last thing I need is a broken tooth. So I stuff it into my armpit to thaw. Then I stumble to the cabin's broken door and hip check it open.

The inside of the shack is musty and cold. I'm thinking I should be outside with the dogs in the weather, but for a moment the cabin walls hold me. I search the stale space for something good.

A piece of rotting plywood serves as a tabletop. There's a bench and an old barrel stove. Its rusted door creaks when I pry it open; there are wads of used toilet paper inside. I wonder if driftwood will burn. The contents of a crushed packet of Top Ramen are strewn over the table; wormy fragments are mixed with old gum wrappers and a cigarette butt. Amid the noodles stands a chipped olive-green candle, its wax splattered on the table's gritty surface. Obscene graffiti is etched into splintered plywood walls—voices of strangers who've been here before me.

This cabin offers me nothing. Admittedly there's a feeble potential for a fire, but I can survive without it. The cracked gray windows obscure any view; the damp, stagnant air makes me shiver. Despite my lips of cardboard and a sour taste in my mouth, I gnaw on the peanut butter granola bar, thinking of the emergency freeze-dried food in my sled. And my bottle of trail mix.

I've got three meals for the dogs along—that gives us some time.

Satisfied that we have enough provisions for now, I sit on the bench, prop my elbows on the table, and rest my face in my hands. For the first time I contend with the question that will consume me for years.

What has gone wrong?

I don't yet understand that there will never be an answer. Surely by identifying the source of our trouble I can fix it, change the outcome. Of course there's a riddle to solve.

As I sit at that grimy table, I'm telling myself that I've never been a musher who pushes too hard. From the conception of my Iditarod dream, my only goal has been to finish the race with healthy dogs. At one checkpoint after another, we've rested longer than any other team. The vets all say my dogs are healthy, happy, and strong. Of course eleven days on the trail have worn us all down, but my huskies are eating and resting. Have the vets been mistaken? What have I missed?

A gust wails, releasing my tears. I taste salt again, this time my own. The bench against the wall invites sleep, so fully clothed for the trail—boots and all—I lie on its hard surface. My eyes close. The storm teases in whistles, and images from the day won't leave me alone: Kanga pulling back and sitting on the snow. Roulette circling to lie down. Spot hanging his head

Kanga.

Sleep comes.

One bark. Then several more cut into the thrum of the wind. I jump to my feet and search for my head lamp. It couldn't be any darker in here. After fumbling around I find it on the wooden platform. Then I try to open the door, which is jammed shut. I kick it open and at last I'm outside, in time to see dog silhouettes coming our way.

Disgusted to have fallen asleep, I fight for focus. I should have made sure everything was ready if a dog team passed, and now I'm a mess. My mittens are indoors along with the dog food cooler. The gang line is tangled because my huskies now sleep in a pile. I can't fix anything fast enough; my swollen fingers are too slow, and this opportunity—to follow another team—might solve our problem.

Hurry, Debbie. You can do it. I'm talking myself up knowing that this might be our big chance.

"Wake up, wake up, everybody." I clap my hands to rouse the dogs, then rush inside to collect my gear. The team trots up the bluff while I'm frantically stuffing things into my sled bag. Creek and Nacho leap to their feet. Lil' Su woofs and so does Spot. They bark the voice of hope.

"Who's there?" I ask. We all wear so many layers, it's difficult to recognize other mushers.

"What the hell are ya doin' here, Debbie? This is one nasty spot." Russ's friendly drawl is unmistakable. Russ and I traveled near each other at the beginning of the Yukon, and more than once he complimented me on my spunky team. His is a motley crew compared with mine. They're laid-back, and travel more slowly than my racy bunch, but they look like Olympians right now.

Russ gets off his runners and talks to his dogs. "Y'all stay now," he tells them. "And don't get no ideas." He walks alongside my sled, shining his light on my mutinous bunch.

"I'll be damned, Debbie. Just look at 'em." His voice is low. "I can't believe your dogs are doing this. Mine have been acting up the entire race. This should be my team, not yours." He offers me a sympathetic shake of his head.

I tell him that they never ran well leaving Shaktoolik, and that all I can figure is that the wind and the white spooked them. Or something about being out on the trail for so long has sapped their spirits. Then I ask if he'd mind if we chase.

"No problem." He sounds upbeat. "I'll pull ahead. Your team has been awesome till now. Straighten 'em out and we'll go together." He moves his team twenty yards forward.

Now I'm awash with nerves, frantic to capitalize on our chance. My heart pounds a drumbeat of expectation that Kanga and Lil' Su are renewed from their rest. I'm fumbling in darkness; everything moves in slow motion. My head hurts and my lips throb. I grab the gang line behind leaders Kanga and Lil' Su and pull the whole line away from the cabin. Roulette and Strider won't stand. They're rag dolls in the wind. Piney and Teton huddle. Lil' Su stands like a statue out front, facing into the gale. Kanga sits next to her and then darts behind, pulling the whole line with her back to the cabin.

"No, Kanga. Damn it. No." I grab her collar and move her out once again. "Stay!"

Now I'm yelling, and she cowers. I switch her into wheel and move Taiga up to lead with Lil' Su. Kanga curls into a defiant knot, as do Roulette and Strider. Spot stands, looking dazed. Nacho pees on Piney. Piney doesn't even mind.

Despite the dogs' body language, I know they can do it. I scold them, telling them to stand up and get ready. Then I sprint to my sled and give Russ a thumbs-up, convinced we'll follow. They might move slowly at first, but of course they'll get going. Never before this day have they ever turned me down. Well, maybe on that one mirrored slough, but that was understandable.

"Hike!" I call in a loud, ringing tone. Russ speaks to his dogs, and they move steadily ahead. In unison mine lie down.

Russ runs back and I meet him at my leaders. "Try it again, Debbie. I can wait," he says.

This time I pat Taiga and Lil' Su, to give them some encouragement. Then I switch a few others and plead with Kanga. It's a charade of desperation.

Momentum doesn't come.

This time I walk to Russ. "You go," I tell him, explaining that I don't want to give his gang any bad ideas. I've heard of circumstances where one team influences the other. It's horrifying enough that my dogs are stopped, but I can't bear the thought of poisoning Russ's team.

"You sure, Debbie? I just can't believe this." Russ sounds so sad. "I'll try anything to help you."

Then he shakes his head. "Damn dogs," he says with a loving, gentle laugh.

I nod.

A squall whips into a funnel alongside us, and when Russ looks ahead, his light illuminates dogs on their feet. He speaks in a low, quiet tone: "Let's go." They move ahead, into the night.

Mine relocate to the lee of the shack and are soon asleep.

Spent from the effort, I walk inside and lie on the bench. Now I've scolded my dogs, been hard on them when they're already down. Snuffed out the last remnants of their trust. For a moment I long for Sydney and Juliet. Then I'm glad they've missed seeing me at my worst. It feels lonely and wrong to be indoors by myself, so I go out and get Kanga. She won't stand, so I pick her up, carry her inside, and put her on the bench alongside me.

I curl up like a fetus alongside my veteran leader. Kanga shivers. Her teeth chatter on every exhale, which brings on my own trembling. One minute I'm praying that my dogs and I will run again, then I'm wondering if prayers ever matter. I consider the possibility that this journey has been jinxed from the start. The endless months of warm and dry weather making training miserable. The snowless winter, a season so mild that rivers didn't freeze. Maybe these were signals that it just wasn't our time.

No. That cannot be. We persevered, and despite the conditions, we logged far more training miles than other rookies. When Andy handed me this legacy two years ago, his message was clear; from his spectacular Iditarod success came the spark for my own adventure.

It's not like these huskies have ever refused to run. They're born with desire for the trail. But not now. After traveling some eight hundred miles, we're stopped less than two hundred from Nome. Where my family is waiting.

Mark and Hannah and Andy believe in us—our run is also their own. Just last night on the phone from Shaktoolik we talked about our upcoming reunion under the burled arch. That was the first time I dared speak of a finish.

"I can't believe we're almost there," I said to Hannah.

Now I see it clearly. My happy dogs charging down Front Street, bright-eyed and eager. The kids waiting at the finish line with wreaths of yellow roses for Kanga and Lil' Su—just like the flowers awarded to the champion's lead dogs.

"Good girls," Hannah will say. "Good dogs. I knew you could do it! Mom, they look so good! You did it!"

Andy, wearing his Iditarod Finisher's belt buckle, will beam. "Hey, Mom, some storm out of Kaltag, eh? I was a little worried . . . So cool." Then he'll add, "You know, now that you've finished Iditarod, you're a real musher like I am."

Then Mark will take me in his arms and hold me. He'll speak, and his voice will crack. "I told you you could do it," he'll say.

The burled-arch finish line in Nome

15

To See Far

Iditarod day 13: Beyond Shaktoolik

At first light, I go out to the dogs. When I clip Kanga back into the line, no one even looks up. The wind is screaming, but my mind is quiet. My plan is set. This is the last time I'll ask them.

I pack my sled, cinch it down, and pull the line of dogs away from the lee of the shack. Then I stroke and praise each friend. Clapping my hands, I walk to the sled runners. In my most encouraging voice I ask my huskies to go.

No way.

The stillness delivers an unwelcome answer.

I return to Lil' Su and Kanga, take them by their collars, and turn the team around. We'll return to Shaktoolik. That's what they've wanted all along.

"Let's go!" I call.

No one budges. Two by two they sit on defiant haunches.

My huskies will not run in either direction.

The wind roars and the shack rattles. Suddenly it feels like everything we've worked for is exposed—like it could all blow away in tiny pieces. We're marooned on the ice twenty miles from Shaktoolik. The dogs won't press on and they won't turn back. And there's not one thing I can do about it.

I have been sitting in the lee of the shack beside them for an hour or so when I hear an unmistakable sound. A half dozen lights bounce toward us over the sunlit white expanse. The snow machines buzz like insects swarming. The dogs sleep, except for Lil' Su, who raises her head. She lets out a single woof.

The wind has died some, but chills zing through me. Crouching at Lil' Su's side, I rest my hand on her back for balance. I want to be steady and strong, but emotionally I'm crashing. Chaos circles in this place where something is ending, and I can't find my footing. The white landscape reels like sea ice no longer frozen.

The noise gets louder. It sounds like dentist drills, several at once. The snow machines roar up the bank, and I stand, all five feet two inches of me, between them and my dogs. These people are intruders. I'm a mother wolf protecting my den.

The engines stop, and several figures walk toward us. A tall man introduces himself and his assumption, "So, Debbie. You're gonna call it, right?"

I recognize him as a trail sweep. He and a group of volunteers travel near the back of the pack and shut down the checkpoints after the final musher passes through. In Eagle Island this fellow advised me to get going, saying my dogs didn't need an eight-hour rest. I didn't bother responding. He didn't know my team. Now I recognize his voice as the one on the phone in Kaltag.

I hope they scratch.

My face flares and my ears ring. He is not welcome here. I'm looking to the side as I answer his question. "Yep, there's really no alternative." The others fidget, and then a long-legged woman struts over to the dogs.

"*Good* dawgs, *good* dawgs, *good* dawgs," she says, her twangy voice going up with "good" and down with "dawgs," like the parrot at the pet store.

Meanwhile the trail sweep talks on his SAT phone. "I'm with her; she's decided to scratch. Nope. Okay, bye."

As he stuffs the phone back into his pocket, he tells me what's what. "So we don't have any time for screwing around, y'understand? We're gonna load your pups into those cargo sleds and haul them back to Shaktoolik. We've got straw for them so they'll be good and comfy. You can ride with one of us. Is that clear?"

"*Good* dawgs. *Good* dawgs. *Good* dawgs," the cowgirl chirps.

"And don't think we'll stop if you need to go to the bathroom or somethin'. Do that now, and do it fast. Got it?"

"*Good* dawgs, *good* dawgs, *good* dawgs."

I tell him I "got it" all right, that these dogs are mine and not his. "We've come more than a few miles, and of course I'm not very happy. Back off and give me a break," I say.

Then I explain that I'll walk to the checkpoint before riding with him, and that my dogs will jump out of those little plastic sleds if they're not adequately secured. If he doesn't have a safe way to carry them, they won't go. Ultimately a kind man who lives near Anchorage tows my sled while I stand on the runners. Another snow machiner carries my gear, so Spot and Kanga can sit in my sled bag. I pat them the entire way.

When we pull alongside the Shaktoolik checkpoint, the communications volunteer comes out to welcome me. He's the friendly man who let me sleep on his cot and made me eggs for breakfast during our brief rest here. Now he gives me a hug and hands me a bucket of warm water and some leftover kibble.

"I'm sorry, Debbie. I know how hard you worked for this." He looks like Santa Claus, without the merriment in his eyes. "Take care of these guys, and when you're ready, come on in. I bet you're hungry. And I'll get you on the phone with your family. They know you've scratched. The banquet is going on right now—they really want to hear your voice."

"Were they really in that plane yesterday?"

"Oh yeah. They landed and stayed here for a while. They know what's happened."

"Is Juliet still here?" I ask, hoping for something good.

"No, she's in Nome with your family," he says.

He walks toward the steps of the building, then turns to add, "But there's a gaggle of kids inside hoping to meet you."

I can't imagine what would make anyone want to meet me right now. "You've got to be kidding," I say.

"You're their hero," he answers.

I don't believe him for a moment. Someday I'll begin to understand the positive underpinnings of defeat, but when I'm standing there fresh off the sea ice the mere suggestion that I am some child's hero is enough to keep me outside. But I must carry on, and I want to talk to Mark. He'll hear my story as if it's his own.

The flight from Shaktoolik to Nome the next day is brief, and the pilot is sympathetic. He smiles at me, says he's sorry, and goes on to explain that this Cessna Caravan usually carries twelve people, but most of the seats have been taken out, making room for my team.

There are four empty seats up front. When I hoist Taiga and Spot into the cabin, they instantly claim two. The others flop in a puppy pile on the floor. I ask the pilot if I can sit on the floor with them, and he says I can. For the first time ever, I don't want to look out the window. We're likely flying over Iditarod's final checkpoints: Koyuk. Elim. White Mountain. Safety. Our last four checkpoints, where our drop bags are waiting. I have no interest in looking at the trail we won't travel.

The takeoff is easy, but Piney and Teton look at me wide-eyed; Kanga is nervous and climbs into my lap. These three are anxious; this is nothing they've done before. Lil' Su, in contrast, leans against the wall of the cabin. She looks miffed, maybe bored. Roulette, Strider, and Nacho cuddle close to one another, alert and trying to resist sleep. Creek is curled in a tight ball.

The hilarious ones are Taiga and Spot. Taiga poses upright in her seat, her head draped over its back like she's lounging at a spa. Spot sits tall. With his snow-white coat and muscled haunches, he noses the frosted window, as if he's looking for something to chase—a ptarmigan or an Arctic hare. He lives only in the present, and this flight is his newest adventure. I wish I could see it that way. He's already forgotten the sea ice. I won't for a very long time.

When the plane drops in altitude, my head fills with pressure. The dogs might not understand that we're about to land, but I do. Our Iditarod journey has come to an unlikely end. And with that ending I'm aware of a new beginning, one that's been in the making all winter: it's Mark's turn now.

I have looked forward all season to passing the Iditarod legacy to my husband—under the arch like Andy did to me. This plan has not exactly been a secret. In January when the stress of the snowless winter mounted and Mark assured me of his support, I agreed to continue as long as he too would run to Nome someday. Because he's a full-time attorney, he would need my help training.

Now it's his turn.

The plane bounces onto the runway with a jolt. Lil' Su leaps up alongside Nacho, who shakes like he's gotten wet. We taxi for a while. Then the pilot shuts down the engine and takes off his headphones.

"Hang on back there. I'll come around and open the door," he says.

I watch him disembark. Then the handle of the side door turns and sunlight pours in. I hear the voices of Andy and Hannah and my sister, Vicky. She's stayed with the family for two weeks now and is in Nome to celebrate my finish. When I hear Mark talking I focus on the dogs.

"Hi, guys," I say to my family. "Take a look inside here!" I want them to see my view, of Kanga nuzzled in my lap, Spot and Taiga in their seats. The rest look charming. If these dogs can make *me* smile, they ought to do at least that much for everyone else.

Andy's head pops inside the cabin, then Hannah's. They fill the cramped space with upbeat chatter. I know we're all nervous. This is not the arrival any of us want. But the dogs are different: they're having fun. This gigantic flying doghouse has reunited them with their family of adoring humans. Tails thump the floor.

"Mom, they look awesome," Andy pronounces. He knows how much that matters.

"They are awesome," I say with a sigh, knowing that only our huskies could make this awkward reunion bearable.

As my children greet their canine friends, it's time for me to move. I step out of the plane. Mark's arms catch me, and he holds me tight.

"Hi, sweetie," he says. The empathy in his voice disarms my resolve to be strong.

"I feel like such a complete loser," I say, burying my wet face in his ruff.

"Well, that's not how we think of you," he answers. I'm still inhaling his response when I pull back and look into his tired blue eyes.

"One thing is certain," I tell him. "Next year's for you."

Mark chuckles. "Don't you speak so fast. You might just need to go again." I tell him that under no circumstances will I run these little troublemakers to Nome next year. I'm speaking with affection for our dogs, while insisting that they are now officially his. After all, this is a family legacy. Some traditions cannot be ignored.

A few weeks later I'm at home in Anchorage, sitting at our messy dining room table. Plates crusted with dried-out spaghetti sauce sit alongside stacks of invoices that need to be filed. A wilted flower arrangement adds to the depressing scene, but the accompanying card is encouraging: *800 miles is an awfully long way to go. Lots of love, Martin and Kathy Buser.* From a four-time Iditarod champion, the words mean a lot.

I'm trying to figure out what to say in a thank-you note to the Busers when a tall stack of letters from schoolchildren distracts me. I tried to read them a few days ago, but their honest voices and candid questions were too much—but I must answer them.

I pick up the first letter. *Dear Debbie, why did you drop out?* The words are penciled beneath a drawing of three striped dogs that look like cats. I glance at the next several notes—only to realize that every single one begins with the same question. Obviously my drama on the sea ice has provided a classroom of third graders in Louisiana with the perfect writing prompt.

One child goes on to elaborate with an encouraging message about doing the best that I could, while several wonder if I feel sad. Another tries a more sophisticated approach, suggesting that I should not give up on my adventure because of failing on the first try.

Then there's a poem that describes me with words like cool, confident, and determined.

Little does she know.

All I know is that I'm tired. And troubled. Surprised that after almost a month at home, each day is a struggle. Of course I have resumed some comfortable habits: my hair is clean, and I've gone back to working out at the gym. I've talked to customers in my school fund-raising business but am not particularly interested in why one was charged more freight than the next. I have tried to gain weight, but my appetite is flat. My fingers have healed, but my nails have a ridge in them by the cuticle, where cell growth must have been affected by the rigors of the trail. I still wake in the night and jump out of bed, begging the dogs to go.

Last night I dreamt of mushing toward the arch on Front Street. Salt was in lead, and just behind him were Kanga and Lil' Su. Morgan and Moxie ran loose alongside us. The kids and Mark cheered us in. I set my snow hook under the burled arch and ran to Salt. I wrapped myself around him, and he sang. I wish I could remember if Kanga joined in.

There's a spring breeze in Anchorage this morning, and as I sit at the table I watch the birch trees sway above the dog yard. We brought ten dogs into town from Denali this week; now they relax in the sunshine atop their houses. Lil' Su's hair ruffles in the breeze. Taiga gnaws on a knucklebone I got from our butcher. Spot's howling, and for once I don't care if the noise bothers the cranky neighbor.

The phone rings, breaking into the doldrums, and it's Hannah calling from college. I know she's checking on me; one more time I tell her that everything is fine. She understands me almost as well as she does herself. She knows things are not to my liking.

The truth is, I've rarely failed at anything; the territory is lonely. Pulling out of a race isn't the crux of my problem. After all, I only wanted to complete Iditarod with healthy and happy dogs. To lose my connection with the team—that is my definition of failure.

While I'm sitting at my dining room table, there's an instant of clarity: I've never left the shelter cabin. I'm there with my dogs, huddled in the lee of its rickety walls. They're cowering in the wind, scratching at grasses, wishing for straw. I'm confused like they are, uncertain where to go. Right now I do not want to move on.

Part 2

Maybe your stumbling
  saves you, and that sound in the night is more than the wind.
    —WILLIAM STAFFORD

Debbie and Sydney

16

Taking Turns

2004 Copper Basin 300: Checkpoint #2, Paxson. January 8

My neck aches and my feet are numb. I haven't slept for thirty-six hours, and that won't change anytime soon. Mark is running the Copper Basin 300, and I am his official handler. That's the way it is: I'm on the sidelines with a cluster of onlookers, pretending to be happy watching my husband take care of the team, but really, I only see our dogs.

Piney's wrist is swollen. Nacho's hoping for a biscuit. Lil' Su looks to me for a massage. They expect me to respond, but I can't. This is a roadside race, where I'm to drive our truck day and night from one checkpoint to the next while Mark mushes the three-hundred-mile course. At checkpoints I'm to clean up after the team leaves and pick up any dropped dogs. Handlers can watch their team while their musher is sleeping, but short of an emergency, we are forbidden to touch the dogs.

So here I am, unable to care for my own. Meanwhile Mark rummages through his handlebar bag searching for matches. Icicles hang from his beard; his eyes look puffy and tired. Even though it's way below zero, he's bare-handed. Just a day and a half into the race, he is already used to the cold.

"Ahhh-ha!" he proclaims with a chuckle. "My Boy Scout match safe! Don't leave home without it."

He holds up the little brass canister and flashes a smile to some volunteers watching. I can't believe he's so jolly. When Teton and Reno ran up the road loose, dragging only a few feet of frayed rope, I stiffened with fear. They had just run a trail notorious for open creek crossings, where sled dogs can panic and chew up equipment or one another. When winter water is involved, mushers need to be vigilant. Mark apparently thinks it's funny, but I want to know how those two got loose.

"Did it happen at the river?" I ask.

"Oh no. That little trickle? That was nothing. Sure, I had to go wading to pull everyone across, but my pants froze so fast, my feet didn't even get wet!"

A thick layer of ice coats his snowsuit halfway up his thigh. Mark walks like the Tin Man needing some oil. He continues to explain that the leaders got loose when he stopped to switch Nacho and Spot.

"When I said, 'Hike,' Reno and Teton took off. I couldn't figure out why the rest of us didn't!"

Mark is so giddy with sleep deprivation, he's not concerned that his swing dogs gnawed the gang line in half. Or that our new, shy leader, Reno, might have panicked in the confusion and fled down the trail.

"No big deal, right, Nacho Bacho?" he adds, patting his favorite boy.

This race is beginning to feel like a big deal to me. He could have been paying closer attention. Anyone knows that loose dogs are in danger, particularly on a trail that crosses the highway. I would be mortified to come to a checkpoint with a team in such disarray, but not my husband. Mark always assumes everything will work out.

Now Nacho fidgets and noses around in the snow. Piney stares at me and holds up her left paw. She knows that I'm about to wrap it and cannot figure out why I haven't. I'm a mother bear locked in a cage.

Mark knows all about my attention to every dog detail. Long ago we agreed that I'm the leading musher and he is the ultimate handler, but this year our roles are reversed. In order to address this challenge, last week we played a lighthearted game of Stump the Musher.

"So, Mark," I said, quizzing him, "which wrist of Piney's gets sore?" He answered correctly but admitted to a fifty-fifty chance. Then came a more important question: "And who has just come into heat?"

"Sydney," he pronounced.

I quickly posed a follow-up question: "So which of our males is still intact: Spot, Nacho, Terry Kern, or Reno?"

"Uh, that would be Spot!" he exclaimed.

"Wrong," I replied. "He was neutered last fall!"

Our game went on for another half hour; he came up with a marginal score. It's not like Mark is incapable of remembering these things. He's an attorney working in a complicated field of regulatory law, but he enjoys a straightforward, easygoing approach to mushing, different from mine. It's a good thing my husband is an earnest student. He's carrying notes from our game on a laminated list inside his pocket.

Now, 150 miles into Copper, he's slept for only an hour. So it's not surprising that he doesn't notice that our new gray youngsters, Topaz and Spur, are busy in wheel. Topaz is nibbling on her coat, and Spur has pulled off two booties. Farther up the line, Taiga is so impatient for her meal that she bites the snow. I clear my throat in a futile attempt to catch Mark's attention. Then Lil' Su stretches her front leg as far as she can, successfully snagging a bag full of salmon. Spot barks, Kanga growls, and I can no longer keep quiet.

"Lil' Su! I know you're hungry, but don't eat that!"

I'm snarling at my leader, trying to prevent bad habits. Really it's Mark's attention I'm after.

"I know, I know. I need to stop talking," he snaps, returning my glare.

I am sorry to have made him angry. The last thing a sleep-deprived musher needs is a critical handler, but I cannot ignore our huskies.

Mark pulls out his list and begins to focus. I glance one more time at Kanga and Lil' Su, Spot, Sydney, and the rest, and then I walk away. If only I could explain to them what's going on—that this is Mark's year and together they'll go to Nome. They need to get there this time. Then next season we'll finish the journey we've begun.

I walk to our Dodge Ram, open the creaky door, and hoist myself in. Despite my long-standing unease with everything mechanical, I've learned a thing or two this winter about the dog truck. Like the importance of cycling the manifold heater five times before turning the key. I do that now, and the diesel engine cranks with an anxious whistle. Then it hiccups into an uneasy rumble. Meanwhile dissonant thoughts rattle through my mind: I am no better suited for this stint as a handler than this truck is meant for the arctic cold. I turn on the heat, and ice-cold air sputters into the cab. The temperature gauge blinks –40, with an ominous *E* alongside. Mark says *E* stands for *error*. Evidently the air temperature is beyond measure. I'm thinking the winter's trials are also.

In the end Mark completes Copper Basin, but it isn't pretty. He stops for ten minutes at Tolsona, twenty miles from the finish, to go inside and fix a failing head lamp. When he returns to the dogs and asks them to continue, they refuse. Kanga sits down in a huff, leading the others into a full-blown mutiny. Mark eventually walks in front of the team. He reports later that it took an hour before they agreed to move down the trail. My husband hallucinates on the way to the finish about For Sale signs that he still swears lined the wilderness trail.

A few weeks after Copper, Mark enters the Tustumena 200, hoping to regain the respect of the team. This time I decide to stay home, leaving the race to the musher and his dogs. They do well for the first 150 miles, and with each report it's apparent that Mark and the team have hit stride. At 11:00 PM I'm elated, driving 200 miles south hoping to be there in time for their triumphant, long-awaited finish—when my cell phone rings.

"Debbie, I just scratched. We've come back to Rockies. They won't run in the wind."

Rockies is the last checkpoint on the race, a mere fifty miles from the finish.

I've just scratched.

I'm thinking the team must be refusing to leave the checkpoint, which is bad enough, when Mark elaborates.

"We left Rockies just fine—but Deb, it's blowing a gale out there. Kanga kept jumping off the trail and into the snowbank. She won't go. I tried everyone up front before returning to the checkpoint."

"No!" I respond.

In an emotional mix of empathy and armchair criticism, I plead with my trail-weary husband, "You must keep going."

I beg him to try anything, even an overnight layover. Another mutiny would compound my own failure on the sea ice.

"They cannot balk again," I say.

But they do.

He calls back within a few hours to say his scratch is official. That they went out again but shut down within a few miles.

"I'm okay with it, Deb," he tells me. "But I've got to say, you can *have* Juliet. I loaded her when she wouldn't go, and when we were finally moving, I look down to see her face popping out of a hole she chewed in the side of my sled bag!"

Now I'm laughing. Juliet has never cooperated for Mark; he's way too matter-of-fact. Of course she'd chew or wriggle her way out of a sled bag, particularly if she's not tired. The image of her little gray head peering at Mark is actually funny, until I hear more.

"I had to put her back onto the line. We went for a while, but when we got back into the wind, Kanga sat down. She's just not cut out for this either."

Kanga. Of course she can do this.

I want to believe in Kanga, but this report haunts me, echoing advice from a friend soon after my scratch: "It only takes one to start a mutiny, Debbie. You need to figure out who it is and take that dog out of your team. Otherwise one bad attitude will affect them all."

Now Mark is suggesting that Kanga's the instigator, a possibility I cannot bear. Yet I admit that there have been hints. On a six-mile run after my scratch, we were within a few miles of our kennel when my seven-dog team sat down. Kanga was in wheel, but I thought I saw her pull back. One quick, subtle jerk on the line. A signal perhaps. But I couldn't know for sure—didn't want to.

Now I wonder.

Mark tells me he's going to sleep off the race at the checkpoint and drive home in the morning. That I should go home and get some rest.

I tell him I'll try, but my busy mind won't let me sleep. I toss and turn, replaying that short run last spring. Sydney and Juliet were leading. Neither one was on the sea ice with me; they'd never balked before. Spot was in wheel with Kanga.

I wonder.

A few days after the Tustumena, Mark and I decide to have dinner at our favorite local restaurant, the Southside Bistro. The waiters and waitresses have become our good friends; the chef often comes out of the kitchen to ask about dog training. We are their heroes. They don't even fault me for my scratch.

Now, in flickering candlelight, I notice uncharacteristic deep circles under Mark's eyes. As I take a swig of Chianti, his voice cuts into the silence. "Deb, I just don't know if I can do this."

All I know is that Iditarod is six weeks away, and we have to do better. I don't want to be hard on Mark—to demoralize him any further—but our dogs have gotten all screwed up. What began as a single balk on the sea ice is turning into a habit. I thought we'd set ourselves up to prevent this by adding new dogs to the team. Soon after my scratch we acquired a leader named Reno, Kanga's two-year-old son. He had just finished the race with another driver.

"He's so shy of people, he can't wait to leave the checkpoints," his musher told me. "He's just what you need."

The dog has a history of charging out of checkpoints, but on this Tustumena, Reno's taken part in a mutiny. So have the other newcomers, Spur and Topaz. This habit could be spreading.

One worry leads to another. After mismanaging my own Iditarod, now I have handed my husband a complicated dog team. Kanga, Lil' Su, Juliet, and Sydney are answering to a rookie part-time musher and a handler ill suited for the job. Our veterans are moody, our new dogs confused. Who can fault them? They deserve better than for us to take turns on Iditarod like two children sharing a coveted toy. Our dogs aren't machines—and neither are we.

But what next? It's not my style to tell Mark what to do, and he's not always inclined to listen. Yet I am far more experienced in long-distance mushing. For once I let go of my Iditarod failure and assume confidence; I know the dogs better than anyone. Mark needs a coach, and there's no one better suited for the job than I am.

Suddenly everything is clear: this is Mark's Iditarod, not mine. This dog team is his alone. He needs someone to map out simple priorities and a weekly schedule. Scratching is not an option. Kanga and Lil' Su and the rest must never balk again.

"Please, Deb. Tell me what to do," he says.

It's so unlike him to beg for my help. Mark is made of logistics and common sense. I'm all about the dogs, their idiosyncrasies and team dynamics. I'm a trainer of animals, not people; to coach my husband has never been part of my marital plan.

I sit a little straighter and my resolve settles. I'm hoping to be up to the challenge. Six weeks to go. That should be enough time for him to connect with this dog team.

Mark taking Spur to the line, 2004 Iditarod start

17

The Shadow of the Arch

2004 Iditarod start: Willow, Alaska. March 7, 10:58 AM

Mark is wearing bib #31. Looking fit and strong, he talks to some wide-eyed young fans and signs a few autographs. Then he retreats into the quiet of the truck cab for a sip of coffee and one last look at his list. Even my happy-go-lucky husband cannot ignore race-day pressure. The 2004 Iditarod start is only a few hours away.

Meanwhile his sixteen dogs, tethered to the side of the Ram, are wagging their tails and pawing one another, entertaining the crowd. Andy and Hannah are back from college. Once again they watch over the team. I study Mark's sled, making sure that the carabiner holding the gang line is locked tight and that none of the necklines are frayed. There are critical details to double-check—and a distracting hype in the air.

Our friend Vern Halter, donning his own race bib, walks up and asks how we're doing. I explain that everything is better and thank him for asking. Then I add, "Good luck. I hope it's your year."

He smiles, greets a few dogs, then opens the truck door to give his old friend Mark some final words of encouragement.

A perennial Iditarod contender for the last decade, Vern has long been our mentor. When Andy was thirteen, Vern took him on his first distance race. Andy came home after the Tug Bar 120 having run through the night with our dogs, something that Mark and I had never experienced. He also returned insistent on running the 150-mile Junior Iditarod, designed to give teens a taste of the long trail. Andy would be eligible the following winter.

Andy was determined, but we faced a few hurdles. We didn't have enough dogs to field a ten-dog team. The eight who lived in our backyard had mastered the flash of ten-mile junior sprints, but they knew little about slow and steady wilderness travel. Vern had the answer: he promised to loan us some huskies and help us learn about long-distance racing.

It was a memorable November evening when Vern delivered Fiddle, Banjo, and Kroto to new pens in our suburban backyard. Within a few days they were running alongside our speedsters Lil' Su, Lucy, Morgan, and Moxie. In the weeks that followed, Vern dropped off a few more, and our family delighted in a new way of mushing. Mark, Bernie, and Andy collaborated on building a new sled. We all worked on sewing one thousand booties. To run to James Lake wasn't long enough, so we ventured to new country where we could follow trails as far as we dared.

Over the next five years Andy and Hannah each completed Junior Iditarod four times. Dogsledding with our teens, Mark and I enjoyed the rewards of navigating unfamiliar terrain. Together we learned patience, forgiveness, and hope from our huskies, who drew us ever onward. The kids left for college, but Vern's interest in our kennel did not end there.

Throughout preparations for my 2003 Iditarod, he lent advice. After our recent dinner at the Bistro, I called Vern and described our troubles. He agreed that our team had developed some bad habits and suggested that Kanga, Juliet, and Piney were too risky for Mark to take on the race. Vern offered to sell us several Iditarod veterans—Snickers, Fang, and Wolf. He also proposed leasing us his accomplished nine-year-old lead dog, Fiddle. After leading Andy's first Junior Iditarod, Fiddle had gone on to perform as one of Vern's best. Now he has come out of retirement to help our team get to Nome. Tethered to the side of our truck, Fiddle wags his tail, waiting for Vern to stop talking.

"Hey, Fiddle. Good boy," Vern says, stroking his beloved old leader. "Save him for when you really need him up front, Mark. If your guys have any hesitation on that coast, Fiddle will straighten them out."

Mark shakes Vern's hand and nods. Then he walks to Snickers and Fang, who stand next to each other wagging their tails in perfect coordinated rhythm. Trail-savvy and honest, they're steady long-distance players. Mark kneels between them and scratches their ears, his eyes shining with emotion.

The team is harnessed and bootied, and an official gives us the ten-minute warning. Time to clip the dogs onto the line.

"Quick, Deb, Spur needs boots!" Mark snaps.

Spur looks away, knowing full well she should not take off her booties. "No, Spur," I tell this sensitive girl who learned a bad habit on Copper Basin.

While Andy runs for more booties, the team parked alongside us erupts in a yipping frenzy. They're about to go to the line. Since Mark's not yet on the runners, our dogs stay relatively calm, which gives me a chance to hug him one last time.

"I love you. Keep it simple. You can do it. I know you can. We'll see you under that arch," I say.

"I love you too," Mark answers, and manages to add a little joke. "Will you still love me if I have a belt buckle and you don't?" I laugh and assure him I will, although the idea of both Moderow men having a coveted Iditarod Finisher's belt buckle before I do is a touchy subject.

An official woman in a neon vest interrupts us. "Let's go," she says.

Mark steps on the runners, and eight people hold on to the gang line. Lil' Su starts barking, and everyone goes nuts. I join my husband on the sled, and we ride tandem toward a crowd of hundreds clustered beneath the familiar Iditarod banner. When the dogs stop, I give Mark's arm a squeeze and step to the side. Hannah and Andy hold leaders Lil' Su and Reno, while I walk the long line to bid each dog good-bye.

"Five . . . four . . . three . . . two . . . one . . . go!"

Hannah lets go of Lil' Su, who catapults into the air. The dogs zoom by me. Lil' Su and Reno. Spur and Sydney. Nacho and Teton. Taiga and Fang. Fiddle, Roulette, Lightning, Topaz, Terry Kern, Snickers. Strider, and Spot. They dig into the snow with force sixteen dogs strong. Half were with me on the sea ice; the others were not.

"And Mark Moderow is off on the Iditarod Trail! Good luck, Mark. See you in Nome!"

The announcer's words slice through the air, and Mark's wide-eyed face flashes by. He looks stunned.

I know I am.

A volunteer grabs me by the arm. "Clear the chute, ma'am. Hurry it up. Another team is coming."

I want to snarl back, but instead I duck under the snow fence and walk away from the crowd. The kids don't see me, and I'm glad. There are some moments a mom cannot share.

I push through the crowd and walk toward the middle of the mile-wide lake. Alone. Holding my breath, I watch our team travel a wide arc. They move beneath an endless blue sky toward the far shore, where a crowd waits to cheer them out of sight.

Breathe, Debbie. Breathe.

With my exhale come tears.

He's on his way. I should be relieved. Why does this feel so bad?

My mind is cluttered with jagged memories. The sea ice out of Shaktoolik. Kanga's blank stare. Lil' Su's tired eyes.

Inhale, steady.

The winter crouches alongside me, and there is so much to explain to the dogs. I had to let them go, with Mark and not me.

I haven't left you. It's not what you think.

Breathe.

I think of the others who don't have this chance: Kanga and Juliet and Piney in their doghouses at home. They're key players on the team, yet they're on the bench sitting out a chance of their short lifetimes. Was this the right thing to do?

That decision is made. Move on.

No more meals with lists and grids filled with training miles. No late-night discussion about schedules or snacking. Or the most efficient sequence of checkpoint chores.

They run along the far end of the lake now. Oh, how I hope they can do this.

I yearn for Salt and his chocolate eyes. For the days when this all was lighthearted fun. When Mark and I, Andy and Hannah, first felt the cool air in our faces and the smooth winding trail underfoot. The little cabin with the porch and the dogs out front, singing. Salt curled on my sleeping bag. Robert Service by candlelight. Hot chocolate. Brandy peaches.

Why did everything get so complicated? When did the stakes become so high?

Within seconds they'll be out of sight. I hold my breath but can't keep it in.

Dear God, keep them safe. And get them to the arch. Not another scratch. They need to succeed. Then we'll go again.

No—don't be selfish. They need to succeed for them, not me.

Breathe.

I want to be on the runners. With Kanga and Lil' Su and Juliet. To complete what we began. Our story stopped in the middle—unfinished. With one more inhale, I watch them run off the lake. No one knows where I am, which is good because they wouldn't understand. I stand there. Alone.

It's just a stupid dog race.

There's a tap on my shoulder. I'm too spent to be startled. "Debbie, are you all right?" A friend of Vern's stands beside me. Diane has a kind, round face, and she gives me a hug.

"No, really I'm not," I respond, too soaked in emotion to pretend.

"I know. I've been watching you. I couldn't let you be by yourself," she says.

"It's been a tough winter," I confess. Then we share a few words about worry for the man and the dogs over the one thousand miles that await them.

A few minutes later, when I walk up to the truck, Andy greets me. "Where've you been, Mom?" he asks. He's sitting on the tailgate with Hannah and some others, drinking a celebratory bottle of red wine.

"Just went for a little walk," I tell him. They hand me a glass, and together we raise a toast to Mark and the team.

A little before midnight, Nome is one big party. The Christmas lights make Front Street look like a carnival; race fans laugh as they meander along the festive sidewalks. Rumor has it that the siren will ring any moment. Mark Moderow is near.

I've been waiting beneath the burled arch with some good friends for over an hour. Finally I decide to stop staring down the street. Long ago at junior finish lines, I learned that if I turned the other way, our team would always run in. Sure enough, someone sees it.

"Look, a head lamp!" she says.

A light is bobbing a few blocks away. Then the siren sounds, ringing away the winter, the dark cloud of my scratch, and the season's worries. Mark and our dogs are on Front Street.

Their run to Nome has been nearly flawless; they'll finish in a respectable twelve days. The 2004 Iditarod will be remembered as the race with perfect conditions: mild weather and a consistent snowy trail. Mark has called a few times, and he's sounded tired but happy. His movement from checkpoint to checkpoint has been steady and strong. I know from updates that he's finishing with nearly all the dogs he started with—an accomplishment of meticulous dog care. I can't wait to see who's in lead.

Now they're close, and the crowd cheers. Mark Nordman stands at my side.

"This will be you in a year, Debbie," he tells me.

Now I see them: Taiga and Lil' Su are up front. They're in a steady trot, with eleven more behind them—all wearing their crimson dog coats. As always, Lil' Su is charging, and Taiga's running just fast enough to keep up. When she sees the race fans, she actually starts pulling. Taiga knows how to work a crowd.

As they run under the arch, I call each dog like never before. Mark sets the hook, walks up the line, and meets me in the middle. He pulls me into a tight hug and won't let go.

"Did you see those old gals? Aren't they the best?" he says. Mark's voice is low and hoarse. He's a bundle of raw emotion. One thousand Iditarod miles have turned him into a blubbery dog lover.

"Did Taiga ever pull?" I'm laughing because she looks so frisky.

"Of course not. She pretty much carried her harness here, but look at her now. She's there when I need her." He wipes her wet face with his filthy work gloves.

A fellow from the local radio station, KNOM, walks up and asks for an interview. The checker needs Mark to sign in. There's the matter of taking off booties and giving each dog a double salmon snack before bedding them down.

Tails wag. Reno rolls in the snow; he even lets a little girl rub his belly. Vern talks to Fiddle, and Hannah gives Lil' Su an extra piece of fish. Mark poses for some photos with his wiggly leaders while I walk up the line praising our huskies. Our Iditarod veterans.

Their finish is my own new chance.

Debbie joking around with Kanga

18

Getting It Right

Fifty degrees below zero. The air is still, the night sky dusted with stars. Head lamps flare in the forest where mushers care for their dogs. The field of forty teams arrived here within a few hours of one another. The top competitors will head toward Paxson quickly. The rest of us will stay longer.

My twelve dogs are done eating. They barked for lamb snacks and gobbled their beef and kibble. Unscathed from the wild seventy-mile run, now they're snug in their coats, curled up on beds of straw. I tell Mark and the kids I'm going inside to sleep for three hours. Mark assures me he will watch the team; he'll make sure Juliet and Sydney don't get any ideas about bolting when other teams take off. My husband is a much happier Copper Basin handler than I was.

As I walk away, the snow crunches underfoot and I hear two mushers talking in the woods. They're not close—at least fifty yards off—but sound carries easily in the deep cold.

"Can you believe the trail? Damn race organization never bothered to set it until today," one says.

"And those guys haven't even shown up in Paxson yet," the other answers.

They have reason to be cranky. Usually snow machiners break out this race trail weeks in advance; then they ride it repeatedly so the snowpack firms up. I'd like to hear more but know better than to get sucked into sour musher-talk. It's critical to stay focused.

My schedule calls for a four-hour rest here. By the time we leave, this mess should be sorted out, and lots of teams will be ahead of us on the trail. I'll decide for myself if it's too rough, that much I've learned. Turning away from the chatter, I head toward the shack designated for sleeping.

When I walk into the dark space I'm enveloped in a cloud of condensation. It's hard to make sense of the room. The floor is covered with mounds, the air rank with snuffling. A white anorak dangles from its hood like a ghost. At the sound of an alarm, someone sighs, rustles upright, and switches on a head lamp. This is a workout room, filled with weight machines and racks of barbells. The waking man gestures that he's leaving, that I can have his spot against the wall.

I don't usually share sleeping space with so many others. In most races, the field spreads out quickly. On any other year at Copper Basin, I'd be here with a few back-of-the-pack mushers, but because of the poor trail no one has dared leave. For now we're stacked here together. I notice Martin Buser snoring at my side; his wet socks hang near my face. When I finally lie down, Martin stands and bumps into the rack of weights over my head. I think about how ironic it would be to survive the rough run here only to die when a twenty-pound disc clubs me in the head.

I have to admit, if only to myself, that it feels absurd to lie on the floor of a filthy room after mushing through brutal cold. I'm racing in a field of thirty-five men and five women, and the organization hasn't even bothered to put in a trail. I'm so dopey-tired that I decide to blame Andy.

"You need to run the toughest qualifier out there, Mom," he blithely announced soon after my 2005 Iditarod sign-up. "That way you'll know how good you really are."

I reminded him that I was already qualified, having run a two-hundred- and a three-hundred-mile race before my eight-hundred-mile 2003 Iditarod.

"Doesn't matter," he responded. "You need to get back out on the horse that threw you."

Never mind that Copper takes place in the darkest season—early January—and the course winds through rough terrain that holds the deepest cold. Or that my twenty-two-year-old son admits he'll never run Copper again. He says it was way too scary.

Even Hannah chimed in about how I should run Copper, reminding me that in a second Iditarod attempt, we had better "get it right." She made sense. After all, this is what we told Mark one short year ago.

Now, in this musky corner, I need to sleep—but I'm wired for action. When I close my eyes scenes from the trail replay: I'm driving the dog team in an icy ditch alongside the highway with semis screaming by. Then comes a ninety-degree turn followed by a plowed driveway to cross. I hit the five-foot ice berm, which tosses my sled into the air and knocks the handlebars from my grasp. The dogs gallop off. Without me.

In a hundred yards the snow hook catches, yanking the team to a stop. I'm granted another chance. Then, twenty miles later, I tip over while rounding a hairpin turn that takes us under the highway. I somehow hang on as the sled bounces off the stanchions of the bridge. All I can see is gravel and ice passing inches from my face. The team stops when I slam into a block of ice the size of a car.

Now I'm battered, but the dogs are just fine. I think of the "pretty girls," Spur and Topaz. On Mark's Iditarod, Spur took her turn in lead, while Topaz ran well in wheel. I'm just getting to know these calm beauties. Right now they snuggle side by side, in a deep and contented sleep. They aren't fazed by our rough run and would never fixate on things they could have done better. I'd like to live like they do.

My hips ache, so I roll onto my side and prop a parka between my knees. The discomfort eases, and my mind begins to quiet—enough so I can think ahead. After a four-hour rest here we'll run seventy miles over the high country to Paxson. We'll finally be away from the highway. It will be warmer in the hills, maybe twenty-five below. Vern Halter says there's a perfect place to camp, just after the first stream crossing.

"It should be spectacular up there tonight, Debbie," he told me at the starting line this morning.

An alarm bleeps, and a musher stumbles out the door. He's followed by several others. A few dogs bark. Then comes a chorus four hundred howls strong. As I lie beneath a canopy of barbells, it's good to know my family is watching the dogs. It sounds like teams will leave soon for Paxson. They'll break out the trail for the rest of us. I set my alarm for midnight and slip it inside my sleeping hat. That way I'll be sure to hear it.

We've been cruising in moonlight over high, rolling hills when Spot woofs. Quickly the team bunches up, and I get off the runners to investigate. Leaders Reno and Sydney, along with swing dogs Taiga and Lil' Su, stand four abreast peering at a creek ten or fifteen feet across. Steam billows over glassy water. The dogs' tails are tucked beneath their bellies. It's not too far to the other bank, but there's plenty of water to spook them. I've been told the crossing isn't very deep, but the dogs don't know that. I have to admit that the thought of getting wet right now isn't exactly appealing.

I reach for Reno, to switch him out of lead, when he takes matters into his own four paws. He bolts fast and hard, taking his twelve comrades past the sled in a 180-degree turn. Luckily the whip of the sled sets the hook hard, and the team stays anchored. The dogs yip and yap, twelve tail-wagging landlubbers delighted with their strategic move.

It's important to act quickly. I clip Juliet in lead alongside Sydney and demote Reno to wheel. Then with Juliet in one hand and Sydney in the other, I turn the team and march the entire line straight into the stream. These huskies loathe water, particularly when it's cold. Like cats in a bathtub, they splash in a frenzy behind me.

I do the best that I can. With frigid water pouring over the top of my boots, there's no choice but to engage in a high-stakes game of arctic tug of war. It's 120-pound Debbie versus twelve athletic sled dogs and a 150-pound fully loaded sled. Because I have Juliet's collar in my hand, she has no choice but to swim. Sydney is forced to follow. Swing dogs Lil' Su and Taiga pull back, meaning little Juliet and Sydney can only tread water. I manage to grab Lil' Su and yank her forward, effectively recruiting another pair for my team. Now Lil' Su, Taiga, Nacho, and Topaz shoot for the far bank—and the peer pressure rises. I yank the gang line and force Fang and Snickers into the water. They leap across like hares. Soon my twelve soggy huskies celebrate on an icy shore.

That the dogs are across is a relief, but my sled is midstream and listing perilously to the side. *It can't tip over.* I splash back to it, and manage to push it up onto the slippery bank, where a spirited brawl is in full swing.

My huskies aren't exactly fighting. They're offended to be all wet, and after a sub-zero dunking, they're possessed with a form of canine ecstasy. Kanga and Lil' Su try to shake off the water. Then they roll in the snow. Juliet and Sydney spin around and around, braiding lines into macramé knots. Zeppy chews loose and slinks into the woods. Reno is terrified and bolts after him. Somehow Taiga takes off her harness. She runs naked down the trail.

Quickly I work to free everyone from the tangle while keeping track of the three fugitives. I take off everyone's booties, which have frozen into ice shoes. It's important to hurry because if another team piles up just behind us, the pandemonium will double.

I catch Zeppy and call for shy Reno. He scampers ahead, just out of reach, proposing a game of Catch Me if You Can. When I pull out a bag of herring snacks, I win. Even smarty Taiga runs to me for the treat. Then I give extras to Fang and Snickers. Patient and cooperative, they have the best manners on the team.

When everyone is back on the line, I call, "Hike." We travel about a mile before I set the hook and pull the team off the trail for a two-hour rest. While the dogs groom, licking ice off frozen fur, I boil hot water for their meal and my own.

We're above tree line; the thermometer I carry on my sled bag shows a balmy minus twenty degrees Fahrenheit. My high-tech boots are filled with water, but my feet aren't cold. I'm wearing mountaineering liners designed for nights like this one. I lie on my back and raise my feet toward the sky. Water pours out of my boots; then I pry them off and change my socks. Even though my pant legs are crusted with ice, I'm remarkably dry.

Within a half hour I'm settled on top of my sled, sipping on hot chocolate while my dogs snooze. I'm pleased that we're on schedule, splitting up an eight-hour run with a two-hour break. We're doing what we learned to do on our long journey to Shaktoolik, tapping into a rhythm the dogs have come to expect. We know this dance by heart.

I turn off my head lamp and burrow deep into my hood, snuggled in satisfaction that we're on the right side of the river. Through the frosted hairs of my wolverine ruff I gaze at the sky dappled with stars. Then there's yipping behind us and a stern male voice. Another musher is coaxing his team across running water.

The sky lightens with dawn; we zip across the road and run downhill into Paxson. The last few hours of trail were riddled with trouble: a deep icy trench on a steep downhill led to a deeper water crossing. A punchy trail proved to be miserable for the dogs. So when I see that familiar gas station surrounded by dog trucks, I'm elated. We have just completed one of the toughest runs in the sport; my little Iditarod mischief-makers have mastered crossing open water. The dogs run right to Mark, Andy, and Hannah. My family looks relieved.

When I step off the runners I can hardly walk. My snowsuit is glazed with ice so thick, my knees can't bend. Opening my sled bag to pull out dog food is impossible—the zipper is frozen shut. Of course, no one is allowed to help me, and so I begin the painstaking process of chipping ice with my Leatherman.

"That's it," I say. "I think we should go to Maui for spring break." Iditarod starts the first weekend of spring break; I'm trying to be funny.

"Really, Mom!" Hannah laughs and apparently likes the idea. She's so bundled up with hats and scarves, I can hardly see her face, but her eyes are merry.

"That might be the best idea ever!" she says.

We tease back and forth, but it occurs to me that long-distance dog racing might be the biggest joke of all. Here I am, having battled open water with twelve dogs through a long sub-zero night, and now in minus thirty degrees Fahrenheit I'm supposed to be happy to spend six hours in a gas station, resting on a greasy floor. I babble about mai tais and waves, sun, and skimpy clothes. I talk about how much money we'll save, going south for a weeklong vacation instead of funding a stupid thousand-mile dog race. Maybe it's because I am so tired that my banter takes a serious turn.

Mark hears trouble. He doesn't like this line of thinking, and scowls. Andy chimes in, "Fine, Mom. Good idea. But before you call Hawaiian Airlines, why don't you feed Juliet? I think she's hungry."

Mark gives me his exasperated look, like he understands there's nothing he could say that would matter. Like I knew there was no use interacting with him last year during Copper. He decides to go indoors and tells the kids to come with him.

"She needs to concentrate," he says.

The boys—the two Moderow Iditarod veterans who have their Finisher belt buckles while I don't—walk away. Hannah lingers, then touches my arm. "Mom, you're doing a good job. Take care of them, and then you get some sleep. The dogs look awesome," she adds.

Mark has permission to be my alarm clock; he wakes me after three hours of sleep. I sit up with that all-over feeling of dog-race yuck: my mouth tastes like a combination of trail mix and Tang. And my lips burn. Maybe this is what it feels like to be a hundred years old.

I ask Mark how the dogs are. He says they're fine and teases that they look a bit better than I do. When I ask him how many teams are still in the checkpoint, he says quite a few but that some are scratching, including Martin. That information wakes me. I can't imagine why Buser would pull out. He is the master who advises rookies never to consider scratching from a dog race unless "there's a bone sticking out."

Mark tells me to forget about Martin. It's obvious my husband does not want me to entertain any ideas about scratching. When I remark that it's critical that the dogs are doing well, he scowls and shakes his head. I respond that the decision is mine. I'll go outside and see how Juliet and Sydney, Kanga, Lil' Su, Reno, Fang, Snickers, and the others look. If they're bummed or sore, then I'll call it off, like the four-time Iditarod champion. I'm telling this to Mark when Andy and Hannah walk in.

They're all very cheery, which only increases my suspicion. I glare, wondering how I got myself into a dog race that includes family advisors. I gather up my things and march out the door. When I'm within a few yards of my sled, Nacho woofs and jumps to his feet. He pees on Taiga, who growls and leaps out of range. Then he wags his tail, and all the rest stand up. Juliet and Sydney stretch, then playfully nose each other. Lil' Su shakes off the frost and gets them all barking.

When Kanga joins in, yipping her piercing high yap, I get the message: Maui will have to wait. This team wants to keep going.

We leave Paxson in darkness. With four or five teams behind us, I'm pleased that we're not the last on the trail. What I don't yet know is that while I was sleeping, more than half of the field scratched, loaded up their dogs, and trucked home. I still think they're mushing on the trail ahead.

I'll find out later that when the trailbreakers left Paxson to snow machine the next run, they broke through thin ice on Paxson Lake. Both machines sank to the bottom; somehow the men managed to crawl to safety. The race was held up for several hours, during which I was still on the incoming trail. By the time I pulled into Paxson, Martin and others had decided that it was too dangerous to proceed. As I slept, mushers pulled out of the race and left. Meanwhile race organizers rerouted the course along the other shore, so the Copper Basin 300 could continue.

My family knows all this while I am in Paxson, but they don't tell me. They fear I will get spooked; they know a scratch in Copper would end my Iditarod journey. So they sit with me while I eat a greasy cheeseburger, and watch while I pack my sled. Years later they maintain that they were confident the new route was safe—after all, several teams successfully crossed the lake while I slept.

At the time I'm oblivious to any danger. Several checkpoints later I ask a race official what place we're in. When he answers, "Fourteenth," I think he's joking—there must be thirty teams ahead of us. He explains that over half the field scratched in Paxson, and tells me why.

"And my family knew this?" I'm incredulous.

"Oh, they knew," he responds. Then he says we have a realistic shot at the top ten, and that my dogs look particularly strong.

The final fifty miles of the race are icy and rough, but nothing will stop us. My huskies have found their cruising speed, and that's all that matters. When we pass through Tolsona, twenty miles before the finish, Kanga is in wheel right in front of the sled. I'm running her there in order to watch her and make sure she doesn't cause any trouble like she did with Mark. This time she's happy and eager. I shout praise to Kanga and the rest as we accelerate away from the checkpoint.

We're only a few hundred yards out of Tolsona when I see a team stopped at the side of the trail. As we approach, the musher hustles to her dogs and stands them up.

"Let's go, let's go!" she shouts.

I hear her desperate call as we pass, and notice her dogs looking glum.

"Come, let's go. Good dogs. Come!" I call praise to her team while slowing my own. When hers don't follow, I try again, but I know we cannot linger. With empathy I call to her, "Take your time, and good luck!" This time mine are the dogs who keep moving.

A few hours later I'm thinking that we must be nearing the Copper Basin finish line when my head lamp burns out. In the black of night we charge down an icy road, and there's nothing I can do to slow the team. I'm standing with both feet on the brake, certain we've gotten off trail, when I see a streetlight next to a chain link fence and a bunch of cars. Bracing for the inevitable crash, I throw my sled on its side, and the dogs drag me full tilt into the parking lot.

Miraculously, the team stops. I look up to see a fellow running toward us from a nearby car.

"Congratulations," the official says. "You've just completed Copper Basin in thirteenth place."

That's when I see our truck. Its lights come on and my family runs over.

"We missed it! Why is your light out?" Hannah asks.

While she and Andy dozed, Mark was in charge of watching for my head lamp on the hill. With no signal of our approach, they all missed my finish. I don't even care.

All that matters is that my huskies and I have crossed a finish line. And after Copper Basin, Iditarod should be easy.

Debbie's drop bags for McGrath

19

Drop Bags

Ten days after Copper, I'm sitting in my living room staring at a pile of Iditarod drop bags folded on a chair. There are sixty-four of them, three for most checkpoints. The bag on the top of the pile reads SHAKTOOLIK; its blue-stenciled letters taunt me, so I find one of the NOME bags and place it on top.

"Take that!" I say.

Mark laughs. "Hell, if I can get there, you can," he responds.

He grabs his briefcase, gives me a kiss, and walks to the door. Before leaving he suggests we work on my trail food that evening. I agree. Drop bags are due in three short weeks. It's time to focus.

By February 15 we will spread the empty sacks in the driveway in a big circle. In the middle we'll pile provisions for the trail. I know from experience that the quantity of dog supplies will be shocking: seven hundred pounds of beef, six hundred of kibble, twenty-five hundred booties, to name a few. Everything will be bundled in small usable parcels. There will be fifty-five one-gallon bags of frozen beef sliced thin like pieces of bread. Thirty-five bags of salmon slices. A hundred and ten quart-sized bags holding five sets of booties in each. My musher supplies will also be plentiful. I'll have packed thirty gallon-sized bags with my own food, and another thirty with personal items such as glove liners, heat packs, batteries, neck gaiters, and socks.

Mark and I will work from a detailed grid, filling each drop bag with items designated for each checkpoint. We'll try to keep everything standard for the first round of packing, then we'll add extras to places that have particular requirements. When all is done and the pile is gone, we'll tie the sacks shut and throw them—all eighteen hundred pounds of them—into a borrowed pickup truck. By 5:00 PM Mark and I will deliver my drop bags to a hangar, to be flown out on the trail. Dinner and Chianti at the Southside Bistro will follow. We'll celebrate our shared victory: preparation for my 2005 Iditarod will be complete.

Today drop bag preparations begin. I've perfected my trail routine; that was proven during Copper Basin. The new challenge is to put my trail system onto paper, then into sixty-four bags that will supply a one-thousand-mile journey. Simple is best, but there are so many variables to consider: storms, severe cold, and even too-warm temperatures that can cause dog and human food to spoil. I'm tempted to send out everything I can possibly need. That's what I did in 2003, and the choices were overwhelming. This year I have to get it right.

So I sit at the dining room table and create a new list, dumping my post-Copper mental inventory onto paper. Each entry is detailed with notes so Mark understands exactly what I'm thinking. Clear communication is key. This is no time for a marital spat.

I think about the dog bowls that cracked in the deep cold during Copper—there's a good challenge for Mark. I write *Dog dishes: find/make/buy?* Then there's an entry for me. *Make and bag muesli.* I'm the chef for that concoction, which includes protein powder, turbinado sugar, eight kinds of grains, and powdered milk. Next are several chores that either of us can handle. *Find and count socks, bag in quan-*

tity specified. I need to have lots of extras. *Figure out what kind of small backup head lamp to carry and get batteries.* That might entail a call to Andy at college. *Bag all batteries in specified categories. Buy chore gloves, liners, matches.* Every detail matters.

Musher hydration is fundamental. I need powdered sports drinks that taste good when hot. *Make drink mixes and figure proportions.* Then a critical issue: *Buy 25 GOOD chocolate bars.* Mark's happy with Snickers and KitKats, but for me it's all about Lindt and Milka, Godiva and Ritter.

Night after night we work from the list. Soon every surface of our house is cluttered with stuff. There are piles of socks, gloves, and heat packs on the dining room table. Muesli, hand wipes, batteries, and chocolate bars consume the living room couch. The kitchen floor is sticky, the counter packed with soups and stews that need to be sealed in meal-sized portions. I try to eat healthy food on the race, and almost everything needs to be frozen. Our freezer fills up, so we keep the rest in boxes on the porch. Then during a warm spell at the end of January everything begins to thaw, so we're forced to rent locker space downtown. Mark takes perishables there every morning on the way to the office.

The list grows every day. *Make necklines, make 10 more tugs, wheel tugs must be a different color, bottle canola oil, find and count cables for dropped dogs. Pick up beef from Dave, order fat, consider herring packaging and quantity.*

Mark and I have prepared for dog races side by side for years. Together we crank through the chores.

One evening, when the deadline is near, Mark consults my scribblings and raises his eyebrows. "Really?" he asks.

I'm counting out fifty bags of trail mix when he reads me the entry: *Consider sending a snowboarding helmet to Finger Lake.*

Mark is always honest, and he doesn't hold back. He claims I'm being ridiculous. No one wears a helmet dog mushing. That would be like a rodeo cowboy going out of the team-roping chute with a helmet on. When I tell him it might make good sense to a fine horseman, he responds that it just isn't done.

Now I'm on the defensive. He's found my soft spot. It's not that I'm afraid of getting hurt, I tell him. I want to feel strong at the top of the Happy River Steps. My goal is to have that "cowabunga, here goes nothing" spirit like his, which perpetuates fine footwork and graceful sled handling. Like my father's "no guts, no glory" bravado. I just want it to go well.

"What's wrong with a helmet if it gives me confidence?" I ask.

Mark has listened to my sled-handling worries for years. He tells me one more time that I'm much better on a sled than he is, and that the mountain range is nothing to fear.

He assures me he'll do some research on helmets but adds, "Remember, you've said so yourself: never try anything for the first time during Iditarod."

Why does he always have to be so damn logical?

Now I envision my goggles getting foggy at the top of the steps because the ruff on my parka and the helmet simply don't go together. I don't want to admit it, but I should have thought about a helmet a long time ago. It might be time to bury my fears and stick with my plan—and stop trying to improve it.

The problem is my rising anxiety. Despite everything going well this season, what if this attempt ends in another scratch? Or worse: what if I crash, endangering the dogs? Suddenly it feels like this whole project has taken on new life, one that is no longer the celebration of a family dog team but rather an obsession of mine to save face. Selfish and ego-driven. Expensive and risky.

Of course there's risk.

The daring voice in my mind responds. *Nothing good in life comes from sitting on the couch being careful.* I've known that forever. Think of what I would have missed if I'd not dared to move to Alaska. Or stayed in Manhattan rather than chase my dream to Wyoming. What if Andy and Hannah hadn't gone in that first junior dog race? What if my parents had been too fearful to try for another child?

I remind myself that there's no turning back. I'm leaving on Iditarod in a few short weeks, and I've done everything possible to prepare. It's not like I have no experience. Over the last five years, I've raced this dog team several thousand miles. Just this season the dogs and I have traveled more than twenty-five hundred. I'm in the best physical shape of my life.

I cross the helmet off my list. There are a host of more important considerations: Buy dog biscuits, different flavors. Count and bag booties, order more mediums if necessary. Count runner plastic. Find foot ointment containers and fill. Count wrist wraps and make more if necessary.

I need to stop fussing around.

Debbie and her dad before her wedding ceremony, 1980

20

Stepping Out

Mountains never used to scare me. When I was young, the steeper the ski slope, the better. Finding the best view of the Absarokas in Wyoming meant riding my quarter horse to the crowned, windy summit of Whiskey Mountain. To climb in Alaska meant to seek the thrill of high alpine adventure.

I trained hard for these challenges and did my best to prepare. But real living came when I stopped anticipating and stepped out. Commitment meant doing a back flip on skis, or moving from Manhattan to Wyoming, visiting Alaska and deciding to relocate there. Happiness could be made with bold moves. Even after the devastating miscarriages, Salt and I ventured back onto the trail.

But over the years something within me changed. Perhaps the precious high stakes of parenthood delivered a message that responsibility required restraint. Maybe during my plunge on Byron Glacier, I really did lose my grace—that self-perpetuating belief in a good outcome. Whatever the reason, when I'm preparing for the 2005 Iditarod, I stumble on the uneven terrain of doubt.

My parents surely knew the tension between the rewards and the dangers of risk. They must have learned how to navigate that place between action and dread. My father always insisted on having a plan. Maybe that was where he rested his fears and drew the strength to push them aside. A plan to my father was a simple design of how something should go, and it didn't mean he wasn't flexible. Dad thought long and hard about how he was going to pull something off, and he prepared with all he had. Then, when unexpected things happened, he adjusted.

My parents took some hard knocks. Dad returned from fighting in World War II dedicated to moving ahead, only to be diagnosed with testicular cancer—at a time when the disease was considered contagious. Evidently he and my mother quickly regrouped. They agreed that Dad should undergo experimental radiation, and then carried on with their dream for a larger family. Against all medical predictions, my mother conceived another child. When the baby died, my parents dared to try again. I took my first breath when they were in their mid-forties. Their flexible resolve got them through.

In autumn 1984, four years after Mark and I married, Dad confronted his final challenge: inoperable colon cancer. Soon after receiving that news, I traveled east to my childhood home with Andy and Hannah, to be at Dad's side. My first night there, my parents and I sat together watching a fire in their New England hearth. As Dad tossed in kindling he'd chopped himself from the pine behind the house, he noticed Mom's tears.

"Don't be sad," he told her. "We've had one hell of a good run. This is just the way the ball bounces." Then he added, "It's just taken a goddamn cockeyed bounce."

I saw my father for the last time a few weeks before he died. It was January 1985. Andy and Hannah were toddlers, and we'd spent another two weeks in Connecticut. Now it was time for us to leave. I had loaded the children and our bags into the car that would take us to the airport and had hugged Mom good-bye—she'd vanished upstairs. We were all ready to go, so I went back inside to say good-bye to my father.

Dad saw me coming and met me on the front step. He stood as straight as his crooked spine let him. It didn't matter that the doorstep was coated with ice; he wore only a flannel shirt and jeans. My father held me tight in the January chill on the slippery ice. I didn't want to let go.

Finally he pulled back, smiled, and gave me a nudge that meant *get going.* I took the hint and turned. Five paces took me over the fieldstone path he'd laid with his own hands, past the lilac he'd recently trimmed. I willed my feet up the two steps made of boulders Dad had carefully chosen and walked toward the waiting car. There wasn't any snow that winter; the air was musky with damp decay. The gravel was loose, and the pebbles crunched underfoot.

My father wanted to project a stoic farewell. Just one day earlier, we had sat on the porch and talked about his death.

"Deb, my time has come," he said. "I've had a good go, and now it's your turn. I don't want you to get hung up on all this. Life is for the living. By God, I love you." Heartfelt words from the man who always met trouble with a plan. Dad meant that my life was waiting.

When I reached the car, I turned to blow him a kiss. He was still there, straining to stand tall. He raised his hand and smiled. As we drove away, he stood on that step, waving.

Nearing the starting line, Iditarod

21

New Start

"Five . . . four . . . three . . . two . . . one . . . go!"

My dogs and I are bound, once again, for Nome. This time the one-thousand-mile Iditarod Trail is covered with snow. The day is bright and temperatures are mild. There are no more lists, no debates about what-ifs. In Dad's lingo: it's a goddamn beautiful day.

This time I'm focused. Today I didn't linger over family good-byes. Instead I hugged Mark and Andy and Hannah and reminded them that I won't call home often. They shouldn't expect to hear from me until I reach Nikolai, on the other side of the Alaska Range. At the starting line I didn't coo to the leaders. Instead, I steadied Sydney and Juliet for a moment and then patted everyone else on my way to the sled. I stood on the runners, awaiting our countdown. I stayed steady and calm.

Now under way—it's been twenty-three months since we stopped on the sea ice—my huskies have settled into their marathon trot. This team of veterans understands that this is Iditarod. Most of them finished with Mark, and many were with me in 2003: Juliet, Lil' Su, Sydney,

Kanga, Nacho, Roulette, Strider, Taiga, Spot, and Zeppy. Several mush-er friends advised me to leave Kanga and the other mutineers behind; they said that they're likely to act up again. I listened respectfully, but their voices did not sway me. We will finish what we began—together.

As the dogs motor along the Deshka River, we pass fans roasting hot dogs on bonfires. Many hold race programs and call out encouragement.

"Go, Debbie! This time you'll make it. Way to go, girl!"

From the media and Iditarod's website, they've followed the story of my scratch. Now they're cheering on the comeback musher. I thank them but wave off the accolades. I need to focus: one mile at a time.

We pull into Skwentna at 12:02 AM, an hour ahead of schedule. This tiny rural community of several dozen residents hosts the checkpoint on the wide Skwentna River. Now the beam of my head lamp illumi-nates action sprawled across an area the size of a football field. Volun-teers scurry about, tending to teams coming and going. Head lamps hover and circle like fireflies.

My light illuminates reflective tape that decorates nearly every-thing out here. There's tape on dog harnesses, trail stakes, and clothing. During this long, dark season, it's a matter of safety. We all sew or glue reflective fabric to anything that will take it.

It looks like at least a dozen teams are resting here. My dogs line up behind another team that's checking in, and a fellow walks over to greet me. "Who do we have here?"

He hands me a pencil for signing in and asks, "You staying or going on?"

"Staying," I reply, "for six or seven hours."

He tells me to follow a volunteer wearing a neon vest. "She'll help you park the team."

Then he points out the stack of drop bags, and some straw and fuel alongside them. He explains that there's a building on the riverbank where mushers can sleep.

I thank him, then gee and haw Juliet and Sydney past resting teams. We park next to a rowdy bunch preparing to leave.

"Don't you get any ideas," I tell Juliet when she begins to gargle and spin. "We're *camping.*"

Juliet cocks her head and looks to me with bulging brown eyes as if to say, "You're kidding." Sydney barks to go, but Kanga gets it and lies down. As soon as I undo their tug lines, they all shift into their well-rehearsed resting mode: they quiet, circle in place, and look to me for straw.

I cut open a bale and pass it out before taking off booties, doling out snacks and a meal. Satisfied that everyone is eating, I look up and notice a distant line of head lamps blinking. A parade of teams approaches. Because sixty-five competitors left the starting line in two-minute intervals, the entire 2005 field is running close together.

Within a few hours everyone will have reached Skwentna. Some will pause here like we do. Others will grab provisions and leave, opting to camp on the trail. A few will push ahead to Finger Lake, leading the charge over the mountains. The race will be on.

When I was thirteen, I was a dedicated ski racer. When race day came, my teammates and I would meet high on the slopes of Vermont's Stratton Mountain to study the course. We'd sideslip the newly set slalom, memorizing each turn and analyzing how best to ski it. We joked around, but this was serious business. The point was to know the course with your eyes shut, so that when your countdown came and you pushed off, you would not need to think. You'd lean just the right way to carve through one turn and into the next. To understand the perfect line was the first calling; the second was to execute it with precision. A fine slalom run was a thing of beauty, if you could pull it off.

As I tend to the dogs in Skwentna, it's as though I'm skiing the first few turns of a carefully studied slalom. We're right on schedule, holding a line composed of principles I've carefully considered: I'll run my own race and ignore everyone else. This time I'll look ahead, never behind, concentrate on one mile at a time. And always focus on the dogs.

Our bond has never been stronger. After Copper Basin and the long training trips that followed, we are reconnected with an intuitive understanding and respect. Kanga doesn't want to run in front anymore, and that's fine with me. Taiga, Lil' Su, Lightning, Spur, Fang, Reno, Sydney, and Juliet are leaders I can count on. They thrive running up front; their confidence boosts my own.

I'm not even afraid of the mountain crossing—not yet. Prepared with a heavier drag than usual, I'll be able to slow the team on the steepest pitches. This sled is our sturdiest, and Mark rebuilt my brakes, putting double carbides on each of its points. I decided against the helmet but have padding on my elbows and knees.

Our schedule is designed to get us safely over the Alaska Range. We'll run the Happy River Steps, Dalzell Gorge, and the Buffalo Tunnels in daylight so I can see what's coming. In the early checkpoints we'll take moderate rests, not too long. That way the dogs should be eager to run but unlikely to charge over steep terrain with too much speed. We've trained all winter with this run-rest tempo in mind.

Most important are my mountain leaders: Lightning and Lil' Su. Honest and tough, they saw this section of trail with Mark. Lightning's easygoing persona tempers Lil' Su's drive so she is willing to slow down. I hate to admit it, even to myself, but I have dreaded the steps and the gorge for years. We were still in the shelter cabin outside of Shaktoolik when I knew that one day we'd face this crossing. But Lil' Su and I have come through all sorts of scrapes together. She understands that I love a good challenge but am not immune from fear. Lightning was born at Martin's when Andy worked there. It's like he's a good-luck token from Andy's Iditarod season.

For a moment I stand with them and scritch their ears. Lil' Su's light-blue eyes speak understanding, and Lightning's nuzzle reassures. Together they'll get us through.

It doesn't take many hours for everything to change. I'm cooking breakfast for the team at 3:00 AM when Lightning wakes up and stands—on three legs. I consult the veterinarian, who flexes Lightning's hips and tells me the issue is in his gastrocnemius muscle, the one that attaches to the Achilles. I know Lightning's race is over.

I am shocked. This always limber boy has not had a moment of soreness all season, but after a short rest his hind end has stiffened. Despite my lack of sleep, I resist getting emotional. Instead, I give Lightning a kiss and take off his harness. The vet walks him to the line of dropped dogs, while I remind myself that this team boasts six additional leaders.

It turns out that dropping Lightning is the first of two setbacks. Ten hours later, a few miles before Finger Lake, Lil' Su shows a slight tick in her gait. With dread rising, I decide to give her a ride. After rearranging the gear in my sled bag, I load Lil' Su. For several miles I drive the sled with one hand while massaging her shoulder with the other. I know how to keep her on the trail.

The vet at Finger Lake is not so sure. He spends a long time with Lil' Su, evaluating her problem. I tell him about her history and how I'll nurse her through like I did in 2003. He looks at me with sad eyes.

"She's not going anywhere this time, Debbie." He continues, "Particularly not over this next section of trail. The steps are in rough shape. Too much soft snow this winter, and snow machiners have gotten stuck out there, leaving lots of holes." He goes on to explain that with each passing team, the trail is getting rougher.

"Just now we got a report about holes the size of cars. You don't want to put her through that. I'm sorry."

My body flushes with alarm, and I ask for some time to think. The vet walks away and I hold my breath. To stay positive and confident is critical; I owe the team that much. But Lil' Su and I have an uncommon alliance. We were to meet the mountains together.

Now I'm going alone.

The thought of leaving Lil' Su behind unleashes an onslaught of worry: I see myself as a second-try rookie, one of those wannabe mushers who might never make it to Nome. The ones the veterans joke about.

Now in my mind the steps are icy and deeply rutted; trees crowd the tight corners that lead to twisting downhill pitches impossible to endure.

I should have brought a helmet.

Suddenly my meticulous plans—the terms of my courage—are gone. *Look at these other mushers.* I'm thinking they're all so strong and wondering what I think I'm doing.

I'm not exactly Superwoman.

I imagine crashing on the steps and the dogs tangling. If we get hung up and another team approaches behind us, we could be in double trouble. Then there's the horrible thought of tipping over and losing the sled because I can't hold on. What if my clumsiness hurts a dog?

My thoughts scream in protest, but a quiet inner voice whispers answers I'm not ready to hear. Sydney and Juliet are my promising young leaders. Reno and Spur as well. These dogs are up for a challenge. I know that much, but I'm not quite open to solutions. Instead I see myself as that stubborn woman, determined to prove she's good enough to get to Nome like her athletic son and husband. My stomach lurches, and I'm hot and shivering at the same time. A man comes over and wants to photograph me feeding my dogs. I'm not myself, and the routine isn't mine. Instead of putting an empty bowl next to each husky and ladling out food, I lay all the bowls on the snow in front of me and fill each one. This is not the way I ever feed. I'm trying to force a smile while he snaps photos.

I am rearranging my sled, trying to muster up my courage, when musher Melanie Shirilla walks over to say hi. She's Iditarod champion Doug Swingley's spunky blond wife. Mel is an Iditarod rookie, running their team of yearlings. She's a fine musher, an elite mid-distance competitor whom I've raced against in Wyoming. When she asks how I'm doing, it's hard to stay composed.

I tell her I have to drop Lil' Su—and that I can't talk about it. She's sympathetic, having just dropped one of her own, but she tries to humor me by saying how exciting it is that we're about to go over the mountains. She says something about "bringing it on." I recognize that she has that invaluable go-for-it spirit that brings on success. I need it, badly, but remember that she's thirty-something and I'm almost fifty. For God's sake, I might be old enough to be her mother.

I must get myself in order.

Mel returns to her team, and we wish each other good luck. The vet checks back with me, and I ask him to take Lil' Su when I'm inside the checkpoint building. He tells me again that he's sorry, and that I'm making the right choice for a special dog. I go indoors and attempt to choke down some food. When I come back, Lil' Su is gone. The sun is behind the hills, and I know that if we want to see the steps in daylight, we had better get moving.

I have talked to several mushers about the trail out of Finger Lake. A friend told me that as soon as you leave the checkpoint, you need to be at your athletic finest. I try to stay calm while signing out, but Juliet and Sydney are spinning with glee up front. Swing dogs Reno and Spur bark and lunge. The checker glances at his watch and pencils in the time: 4:31 PM.

When I'm scribbling my name on that clipboard, I ought to be focused on the upcoming trail. Instead, I'm thinking of Mark and the kids, and how they're surely anxious to see if we leave on schedule. I've vowed not to think about them during this race.

"Forget you're a wife and mother," one mentor told me.

So far I've followed the advice, but now I see Hannah and Andy back at college, nervously checking the online updates. Mark in his Anchorage office. Even he, the non-worrier, will fret when he gets the call from race headquarters that one of our dogs has been dropped and that the paperwork says her name is Lil' Su. Especially since he's already received a message about Lightning.

It takes effort, but I try to say, "Hike" like I mean it. The dogs scramble up a steep, short hill, and then, sure enough, the trail shoots in a jagged descent to Red Lake. My fresh team bounds downhill in elation; in contrast, I'm cramped inside and out. My sled whips around the first twist, and Sydney and Juliet vanish into a hole. Just as they reappear, Reno and Spur drop from sight. Two by two my dogs pop down into and up out of a crater. This all takes a few seconds, but the memory is in slow motion.

By the time wheel dogs Roulette and Strider reach the hole, I brace for my own inevitable plunge. Then those two wheel dogs do something unexpected. They jump to the right edge to avoid it. Their move is one of brilliant self-preservation, but they wallop me in the process. Roulette and Strider's fancy footwork means my sled hits the hole on a diagonal. With one runner on the high side and the other in air, I slam onto my side. I'm immersed in a truck-sized crater when my dogs scramble lickety-split ahead. I'm yanked upright as the team careens down a steep hill.

My shoulders pulse with pain, but I manage to hang on, only to see another hole—this one on a curve that cuts perilously close to a tree. Again the dogs vanish in pairs, then quickly reappear. Smarty Roulette pulls Strider to the side, and I pitch headfirst into the tree well. This time my knuckles hit something hard, and I let go. The sled pops free. I'm on my side—alone. Snow in my face.

"No, no, no. NOOOO!"

I leap up gasping and scramble downhill after my team. As the dogs turn onto the lake, I watch my sled bounce upright onto the runners. Now there's no chance it will slow them. My gorgeous fourteen-dog team lopes along a sweeping left-hand turn. They move in perfect rhythm, pulling a lightened load. As they glide out of sight, I pray out loud to the snow and the trees and the bright blue sky.

Dear God. I'm such an idiot. Keep them safe. Please reunite us. Please don't let anyone get hurt. I promise never to do anything like this again.

Juliet

22

Hallowed Ground

I'm running across the lake, gasping for air, when I hear a motor humming. Sure enough, a small plane on skis flies overhead. For some illogical reason I decide to stop and wave, both arms over my head. The mere possibility that someone can see my dogs has me imagining that maybe he or she could help. I'm hoping for a clue, like a tilt of the wings. Dreaming a mythological sequence in which the pilot sees my dog team, lands on the lake to pick me up, and takes me directly to them. But the plane gains altitude and flies a lazy circle out of sight.

Then the damned silence. Gone is the jangle of collars, the rhythm of huskies running on snow. In the stillness comes a call: the instinct to think clearly. It's a bad choice to keep running, to sprint myself into exhaustion when the dogs could be miles away. Better to pace myself for what could be a very long hike. So I walk as fast as I can on the snow-packed trail patterned with tracks of my dogs.

Step step step.

With each footprint comes a breath.

Inhale exhale inhale exhale.

It's a desperate cadence that fuels my fear of everything going wrong: Zeppy pouncing Spot. Reno panicking—fleeing into the woods to get away from the altercation and tangling the front of the team. In the dark of my imagination, Juliet is choking. Kanga takes out her frustration by going after Sydney, has her by the throat. It must be forty degrees. I'm dressed for a cool sled ride, not a long hike. I'm drenched in worry.

Minutes pass, and my angst settles into a dull ache. Every so often I look behind me, hoping to see another team. Of course no one is coming; when I left Finger Lake I made sure no other musher was stirring. I didn't want another team bearing down on us if we got hung up on the steps. Now I curse my own planning. Realistically, another musher is my best hope—to give me a ride to the dogs.

Step step step.

There's nothing to do but keep walking.

I'm almost off the lake when I hear it. Barking.

Could it be?

I stop to listen. Silence.

Please be barking.

I'm running when I hear it again. If a team is moving, they don't make noise like this—these dogs are stopped. They sound like mine.

Move faster. Damn boots.

Every second counts. Every instant the dogs are hung up could tempt a bigger tangle, or a fight.

Hurry, Debbie. Run.

The drumbeat of my pulse can't go any faster. Sweat drips down my chest. I've thrown my hat off my head; its strings are knotted and catch on my neck while the hat flaps on my back. My gigantic arctic mittens—tied with strings to my anorak armpits—swing at my side. I'm a flailing mess.

The barking grows louder. Now I hear Zeppy's rumble, Kanga's high-pitched yap.

Yes, they are near.

The trail slips off the lake and into the shaded timber. The air is cooler here.

There's my sled. It's upright—the snow hook firmly set on the trunk of a small birch tree. Nothing could be more beautiful.

"Easy now, easy," I say. Now I see the wheel dogs. Strider's standing, her shiny black body wagging; Roulette's on her feet too. She looks at me with her homely elongated nose; it's never been becoming, but right now it's gorgeous. I scramble up the line.

Spot, you mouse-pouncer. Topaz, pretty girl.

She looks at me with that left eye that's mottled blue, and my own eyes water. Spot raises his nose and sounds a high note. Taiga wags at me all pleased with herself, and big furry Wolf stands proudly at her side. I sputter words of thanks. Taiga wants a butt rub, but I'm only halfway up the line and hustle to make sure everyone's okay. Zeppy and Snickers are next; this could be trouble.

Of course Zeppy's chewed both necklines in half, but that's no big deal. At least he hasn't chewed up any dogs. Snickers stands patiently alongside him, while Zeppy looks at me with round innocent eyes.

I speak to my favorite rascal in tones of affection. "You're such a bad boy."

He acknowledges my praise by jerking all seventy-five pounds of himself forward, trying to pull the hook off the tree.

"Zeppy, be good." This time I use my low, ornery voice.

At last the blessed front end of the team is in sight. Somewhere in the midst of my own scattered fright is the realization that every dog is fine. No one is even tangled.

How have we been so lucky?

Kanga confirms my relief; she stands next to Fang, yapping. He consoles me with his calm blue eyes. Reno wags the tip of his tail in his trademark timid fashion, and Spur lowers her head. She won't look at me. She's taken off her booties and knows that's not popular. She nuzzles my leg, and I pat her. Forgiveness is never in question.

I'm reaching for Reno, to reassure him, when Juliet grabs one of my mittens. She has that wild look in her eyes, like she's had too much caffeine. She tugs on the mitten as if trying to pull it off the string. Meanwhile Sydney rolls on her back. It has evidently been big fun at the front of a runaway dog team.

I stand facing my huskies, and in the silence we exchange questions. They wonder where the hell I've been and how soon can we get going. I only want to know what kind of an angel set my snow hook on that tree.

We've been back under way for something like a half hour when I know the Happy River Steps are near. From reading, I recognize trouble coming. We're running through timber along a narrow twisting trail; surely we're at the top of the series of benches that descend over cliffs to the valley below. This is the place where, in his trail notes, veteran Don Bowers advises rookies to say their prayers. He even says something about revising their will.

I'm damp from running and sweating, beginning to shiver when Juliet and Sydney bolt to the left around a big spruce. Then, in pairs, the others follow. For an instant they're heading left downhill, and I'm still traveling to the right. Anticipating a wicked 180-degree turn, I just can't resist: I step hard on the drag. It is a bad choice, and I know it. I'm clawing the handlebar when the sled slams into the tree and then ricochets around it. Facedown and dragging, I brace for a plunge down the first Happy River Step.

Don't let go!

Two seconds . . . five seconds . . . ten. I'm dragging, but there isn't any drop-off.

I raise my head to take a look, and speak to myself out loud: "Debbie, you idiot!"

My sled is on its side, and I'm belly surfing on a perfectly level trail behind my charging Iditarod dog team. I roll onto the hook that bounces alongside me so it catches, then right the sled and move on. I've just crashed on a simple turn because I was *thinking* about the precipices ahead.

Thank God no one is watching.

Sometime within the next few miles we pass the telltale WATCH YOUR ASS sign. All at once everyone's ears go up, and several dogs glance back at me. Then they accelerate around a bend, and I manage to ride out the turn. Tails puff and a few dogs pull back before they surrender to the cliff and vanish. Then my sled pitches downhill.

For me that first step is all about holding on. Curling my fingers tight around the handlebar, I plunge into the descent yelling "Easy!" The steep switchback is only fifty to eighty yards long. It would be manageable in good conditions, but the thirty-some teams ahead of us have left a narrow rut. Worst of all, there's a deep hole in the midst of the drop-off. Two by two, the dogs scramble into the crater and out. Then they claw the ground in an attempt to get decent footing and launch again out of sight.

When wheel dogs Strider and Roulette get to the crater, again they try to avoid it. I tip over, my arms yank tight and my grip holds. Then I'm up and out. Immediately there's another turn—or maybe there isn't—but another hole gobbles the dogs and spits them out.

This time I yell. "Roulette and Strider, straight ahead!" They think about it, but at the last second they hop like rabbits to the side. Again, I'm over—and manage to hold on. The inevitable jolt follows. The pain in my shoulders steals a breath. Then I'm upright and out. We slam another thirty yards to the bottom of the chute.

One step is over. And it was anything but "happy."

Two to go, or so I was told. In a blink we come to another corner. I'm feeling up to it, and the dogs look primed. Their heads are high, necks elongated, as if they all know this is the big league. Juliet and Sydney dart into the sharp turn. This time I don't let my feet touch the drag. I've just rounded that bend when I see the start of the pitch. And an enormous crater flanked by a tree. It's the same sequence. Each set of dogs jumps in and then scrambles out. I try to steer the sled wide, in order to miss the tree. I'm figuring Roulette and Strider's shenanigans might help this time, but at the last minute they balk. They actually pull back and try to stop. Of course momentum works against them, but their hesitation makes my sled jolt to the right and then hard to the left. As the nose of the sled implants itself on the wrong side of the tree, we lurch to a violent stop. I'm facedown in a hole.

When I look up, Roulette and Strider are peering back at me. Right ahead of them the other twelve are suspended over the steep descent. My sled is stuck on a tree, and I'm not sure how I can free it when fourteen dogs are pulling downhill. Efficiency is my best hope, and I manage to move fast. I set both hooks, then leap to the first two pairs and undo their tug lines from their harnesses. This relieves some of the tension on the gang line, enough so I can pull the sled backward off the tree.

Somehow I'm strong enough to do it and quick enough to pull the hooks out of the snow and stow them in the sled as we launch into an airy descent. There's a landing and then a blur of tight turns. Then I sense another step is approaching. I'm aware that it must be done.

That corner is tight. I can't recall if it goes right or left, but the pitch is severe and the dogs are half running, half scrambling. I'm on my feet. This time I ride it until the end, and when the trail levels, we're on the valley floor. The Happy River Steps are behind us.

I stand on the brake, stop the team, and lean over the handlebars for support because my legs are giving out and every part of me is trembling. My fourteen dogs bark and wag their tails. I need to find my balance.

We reach the sixty-five-hundred-foot-high Rainy Pass checkpoint in the dark of night. The race judge greets me. After he shines his light onto the dogs, my sled, and then me, he grins and says it looks like we've come through relatively unscathed. I joke about my battering and ask him how bad my face looks.

"Compared to a few others, you look just fine," he answers.

Shining his head lamp past a few markers, he points out piles of drop bags and straw. "This year we've put up the perfect wall tent for mushers," he explains. "It's warm and comfortable for a good rest, Debbie," he tells me.

I have no intention of using it. Nothing will take me away from the team. I'll feed them and make sure everyone is sound, then get into my sled for a four-hour nap. I want to be with my huskies, not with a bunch of mushers complaining about the rough trail.

I know the games mushers play. Veterans in that tent will scare rookies with stories about the upcoming Dalzell Gorge. I won't subject myself to that distraction. Our run from Finger was brutal, but we made it. We're together. The dogs are strong. One milestone is behind us; there's another ahead. We're fully committed.

We leave Rainy Pass on schedule at 7:00 AM. At first I don't turn on my head lamp, but when Sydney and Juliet have trouble finding the trail, I switch it on. Quickly they notice the sparkle of reflective tape on trail laths. They run to the first marker and look for the next. In the blue light of dawn, we're on our way.

It takes only a few minutes for the sky to lighten, and I realize we're following a ridgeline above a lake. Then we turn toward a yawning alpine valley flanked by massive peaks. My eyes widen at the scale of this place. We're in the heart of the Alaska Range, traveling North America's highest terrain. Suddenly I'm awash in awe that my dogs and I have come here. The messy run to Rainy Pass no longer matters. This mile—this dawn—is everything.

We cruise along, first skimming the tree line, and then, climbing higher, we ascend a crease formed at the intersection of two bald mountains. The trail is windswept here, allowing the dogs relief from the soft rutted miles we've completed. As we gain altitude I look to the horizon where the peaks meet the sky. That line between earth and air rises and falls like a song.

We've been traversing the high valley for less than thirty minutes when the sun spotlights the highest summits, accentuating multiple ridgelines where I thought there was only one. It's almost too much to fathom—the swing from night to day that illuminates the craggy dimensions of this wildness. I look from the snow-swept mountaintops to cornices curled like waves, then down gullies scoured clean by avalanches. With my eyes I trace the white undulating hills that reach in every direction over miles and miles of untracked land. Then I shift attention to the dogs and whisper their names.

Sydney. Juliet. Spur. Reno. Fang. Snickers.

I talk to each husky as if that dog is my one and only. It sounds like a one-way conversation, but we know better.

Taiga. Kanga. Zeppelin. Wolf. Spot. Topaz. Strider. Roulette.

After a while there's nothing more to say, so we share the silence. Mesmerized by their rhythmic breathing, I lose myself in their feathered tails and muscled haunches. They're prancing, like they know we're traveling hallowed ground.

The run that begins with dawn's promise turns into an extended thrashing. Wheel dogs Roulette and Strider consistently refuse to jump straight into the craters, and within a few miles I crash into a dozen enormous holes. Finally I decide to try Spot and Topaz in wheel. It's a whole new experience.

Looking back, I don't know why it took me so long to recognize the importance of a good wheel dog. With quick footwork and dedication to my well-being, Spot and Topaz agree to meet each hole straight on. This helps me stay upright. Still, with each unavoidable yanking, the pain in my shoulders stabs. As my arms weaken, so do my sled-handling skills. And within an hour or so, I know the Dalzell Gorge must be near.

I'm feeling like a loser—a clumsy and inept musher—when a helicopter buzzes overhead. *Thwap thwap thwap.* A film crew is following the race, and it's hard to imagine they'd want to film me. For a moment I wonder if someone's hurt in the gorge, drawing the media's interest in sensation. Or maybe they hope to catch a back-of-the-pack musher crashing down the drop-off. None of these possibilities is good, but that last one makes me mad.

They want to film me crashing.

The next few turns of the trail take forever—all while the helicopter hovers ever closer. It's a monstrous insect whose pulse mixes with mine. A sharp turn pulls the dogs to the right, and they disappear.

Two by two by two.

This is another place I've dreaded: the two-hundred-foot drop-off into the gorge.

"Don't worry, Debbie, you just have to hang on. It's much steeper and longer than any of the steps, but it's straight." Mark's words ring in my mind but offer little consolation when my shoulders feel broken and my hand strength is spent.

I have to hold on.

The chopper hovers so close, I see the camera dangling beneath it. The menace in the sky beats the air as we pitch over the cliff.

Determined not to give them any footage, I stay on my feet and keep the sled upright until it finally thuds into a deep rut at the bottom. Standing on my drag with its many carbides, we skitter to a stop. I throw my hooks into the ground and wave my arms above my head. Victorious. Then with my middle fingers concealed in mittens, I give the chopper the gesture of my choice—with both hands. Then I toss each dog two celebratory herring.

During the final miles of the run to Rohn, the Iditarod Trail winds through a canyon called Dalzell Gorge. For several weeks before the race, volunteers establish a trail there by building snow and ice bridges that span a creek that runs open all winter. As long as temperatures remain cold, the bridges stay strong. The trick is to keep your sled on track as the dogs weave from bank to bank. This year the weather is mild; daily temperatures have risen above thirty-two degrees. Whether the bridges have melted or not, it's time for the gorge.

Entering Dalzell by dogsled is to ride into an enchanted landscape. The dogs trot effortlessly into the shade of a steep rock canyon. Frozen waterfalls hang from sheer granite walls. Massive icicles glisten in the filtered morning light. The beauty stuns, so I decide to stop and look around. We've only paused for a moment when I hear the faint hum of the helicopter again and a rousing chorus of barking. Spot and Kanga start lunging, and quickly all fourteen are crazed by the canine call. With sight-seeing no longer an option, I pull the hook and we're off.

The team is frisky but I am not. Only during Iditarod would I choose to run fourteen dogs in a place like this. With each pair comes a gang line section ten feet long. The long span from my sled to the leaders compounds the challenge to keep my runners on the narrowing, melting trail. For the next forty minutes it's all I can do to keep myself and the sled out of the water. Repeatedly the dogs zip over slumping snow bridges; I crash often, once ending up on a precarious tilt that leaves me a few inches above the flowing creek. This time I have to unpack my sled, effectively lightening the load so I can push it uphill away from the water. It's twenty minutes before we're back under way, but at least we're dry.

We've been negotiating the turns in the gorge forever, it seems, when the sound of barking nears. The team has been yapping for at least an hour, and I'm wondering if someone is hurt when we pull up behind a tall man leaning over a tangle of dogs. I recognize a fellow rookie, Phil.

"What's up?" I ask him.

Looking dejected, he utters one word: "Love."

Evidently an unscheduled breeding is under way. The canine act can take a half hour or longer. He has no choice but to wait it out. The uninvolved males in the team are jealous, and Phil reports he's broken up a few fights. There's not enough room to pass, so we too are at the mercy of romance's timetable. For what seems like forever, I stand alongside Zeppy and Kanga—they need my company in order to behave. After a while, Phil pulls his dogs to the side so we can pass. Spot makes a valiant effort to get in on the action as we run by, but the others pull him along. Within a few minutes I hear yelling, and then more barking. Later Phil tells me that his troubles had only begun.

Once back underway, I realize we're not far from the Rohn checkpoint. We travel a few miles along gravel bars on the wide Tatina River before weaving into the tall forest and pulling alongside an old cabin with smoke coming out of its chimney. A hand-hewn sign over the door greets us: WELCOME TO ROHN. We park alongside a dozen or so teams, resting quietly in a grove of towering spruce trees.

Built in the 1920s, the Rohn Roadhouse was a popular resting place for miners as they traveled to Alaska's interior goldfields. I'm thinking of the gritty characters who used to stay here, when a familiar figure swaggers out the door. There he is: the trail sweep who sniped at me on the sea ice outside of Shaktoolik. He sees me, then slinks around the corner. My dogs and I rest in the checkpoint for six hours. We never see him again.

We leave Rohn in late afternoon. Within several hours we've bumped our way through the rough grazing land known as the Buffalo Tunnels. There are signs of the herd everywhere: hoofprints, tufts of gnawed grasses, and hot, steaming poop. The air is heavy with the scent of barnyard, but we don't see one buffalo. As darkness comes, the trail levels, and we run through a burnt-out forest. This is the Farewell Burn, an area ravaged by fire in the 1970s. It might be monotonous, but the scorched remnants of trees are welcome proof that the Alaska Range is behind us.

The sun is dipping behind the mountains when I stop the team, walk to leaders Reno and Sydney, and turn to look back where we've traveled. Cloaked in a rosy shroud of alpenglow, the Alaska Range appears gentle, even benign. Despite a heavy ache of marathon fatigue, my spirit is light and peaceful, suspended like the wisps of clouds overhead. I toss each dog a hunk of beaver and treat myself to a Godiva chocolate bar with almonds.

We made it.

Bound in love with my huskies, I know where we stand. The Happy River Steps, the Dalzell Gorge, the helicopter in the sky, the trail sweep, and the Buffalo Tunnels are behind us. So are my fears. Now that we've endured the first third of the Iditarod Trail, I'm able to see her full promise. It does not matter how many miles we still have to travel, and it makes no difference that there are no guarantees we'll reach Nome. This is our place. Our time. I'm burying my face in Spur's soft neck when Juliet gargles, telling me to get going.

Debbie and Do Clarke with their guide Todd,
fishing the Tikchik River

23

Deep Water

My mother was familiar with that place that hovers between daring and doubt. I can still see her at the end of a long day fishing, casting her tiny dry fly—a royal coachman—into the dark water of the Neversink River. I was young, maybe ten, and too short to wade into the deep Otter Pool. Mom decided to give it a try, while I watched her from shore.

Her small five-foot-three frame teetered midstream, where she paused in the strong current and tried to secure her footing. With the water lapping against the top of her chest waders, that top third of my little mother did the impossible. She lifted her right arm to the sky and cast the long, graceful yellow line, dropping it with a whisper atop the mysterious current that ambled against the far cutbank. Mom looked at me with raised eyebrows and puckered her lips as if to say "ooooh." She knew it was a perfect cast, that the water might erupt when an enormous brown trout slurped her fly off the surface. She also knew that with one more step she might go swimming.

I have no recollection if she caught the big brown on that day or another, but I do know that Mom was always at her finest when the fishing got tricky. The possibility that she could wade deep enough to cast the distance charged my mother with joy. If she could just get there, a wonderful thing *might* happen. That chance held her in a glorious place. For a good hour—or maybe it was ten minutes—she fished, and I watched. Time slowed and we both surrendered, captivated by Otter Pool's shining water.

I was lucky to be my mother's daughter, privileged to be her final fishing partner after Dad died. The first year after his death, Mom couldn't bear to fish without him; after that she made an annual angling pilgrimage to Alaska. She would spend one week with our family, and then, for a second week, she'd take me to a fishing lodge in western Alaska, where we cast from either end of a small boat for wild rainbow trout.

The last time Mom and I visited Tikchik Narrows Lodge, the year was 1997. She was eighty-three years old. After weathering several health scares, Mom had almost canceled the trip. In the end she dared to go—it wasn't like her to give up.

The last day of our week together was cold and rainy. Many of the guests elected to stay indoors by the fire. Not my mother. At 7:30 AM, donning multiple layers of fleece, Gore-Tex, and neoprene, we staggered from our cabin down the rocky path to the dock. Our favorite guide, Todd, greeted us there with the boat motor already running. Quickly Todd stowed our gear and helped Mom into her seat. Then we set out for an hourlong boat ride across the lake and up the Tikchik River.

Todd stood as he steered, while Mom and I sat side by side in the bow facing him. It couldn't have been warmer than thirty-five degrees; ice-cold rain pelted our backs as we motored across the lake's choppy surface. Grateful for the warmth of waders on my legs, I burrowed deep inside my three jackets. Watching water trickle off my hood and onto my lap, I wondered how long we would fish in such bone-chilling misery. Then I glanced at Mom. Her eyes twinkled beneath the brim of her soaked crimson and white Norwegian ski hat. Suddenly she straightened and pointed to shore. A lone caribou pranced along the beach, escorting us off the lake and into the mouth of the river.

The ride across the lake had been dramatic, but our boat ride up-river was rough. The water was high after several days of rain, and the feeder streams poured mocha brown into the Tikchik. Todd scanned the current upstream, steering us into the smoothest channel. After a while I turned in my seat to look ahead. The cold rain stung my cheeks, but the discomfort didn't matter. I was pretty sure this would be my last day fishing with Mom.

I wanted to watch the river.

After an hour running upstream, Todd cut the motor. The water rushed, and a salmon tail-slapped the river's surface.

"You're home, Do," Todd said.

Mom shrugged her shoulders up to her ears, and with the body language of a young child she exclaimed, "Oh, it's just *wonderful* to be here!"

"Are you warm enough?" Todd asked, looking for assurance that his client would survive.

"Of course!" she exclaimed. "But I'm not exactly sweating. Come on, Debbie, let's catch a fish!" She grinned and gave me a wet wink.

We fished for eight hours, with a ten-minute break for a soggy roast beef sandwich. With Todd on the oars, we floated downstream casting from each end of the boat. Sometimes we motored upriver; every so often Todd waded the Tikchik while holding on to the boat's gunwales, positioning us over pockets of water most likely to hold rainbow trout.

Mom was a fish snob. She took little pride in landing Arctic grayling; she claimed that these "sailfish" didn't put up much of a fight. She spoke disparagingly of pink salmon, which she nicknamed "cat food."

Only wild Alaskan rainbow trout satisfied her. She fished tirelessly in pursuit of her beloved species.

When Todd announced "one last cast," for the tenth time that afternoon, my mother's arm jerked high in the air. Shedding beads of water, her amber line flashed tight, and a rainbow shot high over the riffle. Mom's gnarled arthritic knuckles clawed the rod handle as she fought her catch, while Todd controlled the boat. His resolve matched hers, and after a good fifteen minutes he netted her twenty-four-inch rainbow. Todd, Mom, and the fish posed while I snapped a photo. Then she held the trout gently and released it into the current. I pulled Mom's flask of Grand Marnier out of the wet tackle box, and we drank a toast to the river, before motoring through wind-whipped waters back to the lodge.

That was Mom's last rainbow, but as her health faltered she managed one final visit to Alaska. She arrived in Anchorage two days before the start of the 1998 Iditarod. In a fund-raising "Iditarider" auction, she had purchased a ride inside a musher's sled for the first ten miles of the race. All bundled up, she proudly sat in Vern Halter's sled as his dog team charged to the starting line. As they took off on Anchorage's Fourth Avenue, she waved to the crowds like a rodeo queen. A quarter mile later, the course followed a ninety-degree turn onto a street called Cordova. Fans lined the intersection, hoping to watch a musher spill. I saw a rooster tail of snow as they rounded the bend. I hoped for the best. Mom might have been the oldest Iditarider ever.

Mark and I met up with them ten miles later, where the riders bid their dog teams farewell. As soon as she saw us, Mom babbled with glee. "We went so fast around that corner, we almost crashed! It was wonderful!" she said.

"Yeah, Mom, I bet it was exciting." I couldn't imagine that the turn had been all that threatening.

I raised my eyebrows at Vern. "Did you try to dump her?" He answered with a chuckle. Knowing that other teams would soon appear, Mark encouraged Mom to climb out of the sled.

"Hand me your arm, Do, I'll help you out," he offered.

"There is absolutely *nothing* wrong with my arm!" she replied.

The following morning I picked up the *Anchorage Daily News* from our doorstep. The front page of the paper featured a photo of my ancient mother seated in a sled tipped thirty degrees off the ground, with a threatening steel snow hook hovering in the air an inch from her face. That's when I knew her report about the Cordova corner had been no "fish tale."

It was autumn of 2000. Hannah and I had just hooked up a dog team in front of the four-wheeler for a fall training run in Denali when the phone call came. Ruby, Mom's nurse, carefully told me that my mother wouldn't live much longer. At eighty-six years of age, she had suffered a series of strokes, so I shouldn't have been surprised. Ruby reported that over the past several days a bad case of gangrene had set in. I asked her how quickly I needed to get there.

"Your mom's not going anywhere until you come, Debbie. She's traveling, but you take your time. She'll wait for you."

After hanging up, I walked out of the cabin and looked at my dogs, wagging their tails. The team was fully harnessed, the four-wheeler running. So I took them on a short run.

Maybe it's because I was aware that the foundation of my life was changing that I remember the run in detail: first snaking through the scrubby black spruce, then blasting through a deep puddle that had melted in the early-morning sun. The dogs' long strides splattered my face with mud that mixed with tears.

My huskies weren't affected by my sorrow. Cooled and eager, they blithely loped ahead. Sometime on that run, Taiga and Spot pounced on a spruce grouse that clucked on the trail's edge. The bird was in no danger—those two weren't wily hunters—but the chase heightened their fun. We zipped over tree roots and around tight corners before cruising into an open area encircled by towering cottonwoods that swayed in the breeze.

We often stopped in the swampy meadow. The dogs loved to roll in its hummocks. That morning I turned off the four-wheeler, closed my eyes, and drew in the musky scent of autumn's decay—a signpost on the road toward winter. I knew that within days I would travel home to Connecticut and that my next run with these dogs would be different. We'd likely sled across this place on a silent, snow-covered trail. And my mother would be gone.

Two days later my plane landed at New York's LaGuardia Airport. A friend met me there and drove me home, where I walked to the side of Mom's bed. She opened her eyes and through gurgled breaths attempted to smile. I held her curled hand.

"Let go," I offered. "Like Dad and you always said, 'No guts, no glory.' God knows you've had one magnificent ride, and you've seen lots of glory. Let go, Mom, it's okay. I love you."

Then something deep within me sparked and began to implode. As much as I never wanted to leave her, I could not linger. It was as if a force drew me to the door of her bedroom, next to the chair where Dad always sat to lace up his shoes. Then I walked on the braided rug in the hall and down the worn pine staircase. My footsteps landed in the same rhythm I heard as a little girl, snuggled in bed, when Mom went downstairs to cook breakfast.

Out the front door, over the uneven fieldstone path of my childhood I fled, past the fall chrysanthemums, into the front seat of my brother Pete's car. He and I went to a coffee shop before returning home to spend more time with Mom.

She had no more time.

Mom died when we were driving back up the driveway. I was sipping the last of my skim milk cappuccino.

Cruising with the 2005 team

24

Trail Friend

We're taking a short break on the trail, having checked in and out of Ophir. Most of the dogs look content, relishing a midafternoon siesta.

Not Juliet.

She's sitting upright, glowering at me like a mad little mouse. Her gray, wet ears droop next to her skinny, white face; her tail is tucked under her belly. I tell her it is not my fault that it's raining, that she should take a hint from Fang. Mr. Make the Best of Anything has uncovered a tuft of tundra, and he's curled up, snoozing away the Iditarod downpour.

Juliet has no intention of napping. I admit that the conditions are not exactly appealing, but I have a good idea: her personal sleeping bag is stowed in the toe of my sled. This recent creation is intended to keep her happy in the cold arctic wind. I've never considered the possibility that it might come in handy during a rain squall, but it's worth a try. I pull the blue bag out and open it alongside her. She looks at me and cocks her soggy head, then dives in nose first. She circles once, then lies down. When she wags her tail the bag wiggles.

Now that Juliet is happy, I can tend to my own troubles. I find a garbage sack, rip holes in it for my head and arms so I can use it as a raincoat. That's the best I can do to stay dry during this two-hour break. Normally it wouldn't make sense to stop in this weather, but there are seventy long miles between here and the checkpoint of Iditarod. Resting is the right thing to do.

About an hour later the rain changes to hail. I'm sitting on my sled, munching on some salmon jerky and studying little ice balls bouncing off my pants, when Spot woofs. I look up to see Melanie and her long line of dogs veering off the trail toward us, their ruffled tails blowing sideways in the wind. Back in McGrath, during our twenty-four-hour layover, Mel and I heard that the miles to the Iditarod checkpoint were particularly slow and punchy—and loaded with holes.

"There's at least eight feet of snow out there," the race judge told us. "You gals should pair up, give it a go together."

I've always been reluctant to coordinate with another musher, but in McGrath, Mel convinced me otherwise. She proposed that we alternate going first through tricky terrain, explaining that her younger dogs have more enthusiasm than confidence. To follow my team would help hers focus. For mine, chasing would alleviate the monotonous pressure of route finding. She made good sense: traveling together might ensure that both teams stay happy.

Now Mel snacks her dogs while I bootie mine, and then we take off. My huskies run close behind hers, following the trail that winds up the Innoko River valley toward the Beaver Mountain Pass.

We've been pushing uphill for a half hour when the wind intensifies. A gust whistles, and I'm surprised to watch Mel's dogs cower. Her kennel is known as one of the strongest in the sport, and Mel herself is an acclaimed musher. I first met Mel when we both participated in Wyoming's premier dogsledding event, the five-hundred-mile (now shorter) International Pedigree Stage Stop Sled Dog Race. She was a top contender, vying for the win while I hoped to finish in the middle of the pack. Mom had just died. I took our dogs to Wyoming in her honor, longing to reclaim my broken spirit.

Our Denali friend and neighbor, Iditarod champion Jeff King, loaned Kanga to me for that race. He wanted his talented short-coated dog to go somewhere warm and get in some happy high-altitude miles before he took her on Iditarod. Kanga upped the performance of my team in every way. She led every mile of my 2001 Stage Stop, guiding my huskies over the sun-soaked mountain passes I'd first known riding horses with my parents. With Kanga's drive up front, we finished in a respectable fourteenth place. Mel came in second that year. She returned the following season to claim her first Stage Stop win.

Now, five hundred miles into Iditarod, I'm following this accomplished champion up an Alaskan mountain pass, and her team begins to falter. My dogs are feeling just fine. They bark like they want to show Mel's team what it takes. I don't know what to think. This weather is ugly. The gusts are at least as strong as they were on the sea ice in 2003. As I'm imagining that there's no way my dogs will move into the gale better than Mel's, hers bunch up and stop. She turns and waves us by.

The wind envelops us. It takes me a moment to think clearly. Reno and Juliet are up front; they're not exactly the bravest. Kanga's behind them in swing, and if she'd just agree to lead, her vast experience might get us through.

What if she's unwilling?

A gust catches my sled, and Roulette circles, preparing to nest. Knowing we need to move quickly or not at all, I leave the pairings as they are.

"On by, Reno and Juliet! On by!" I call.

We careen around Mel, and I crouch low on the runners to be small against the monstrous wind. We move past a lone cluster of trees, and then we climb toward a fully exposed ridgeline. The dogs lower their heads and trudge onward. Every twenty-five yards or so I glance back to make sure Mel's team is moving. At some point they hesitate, so I kneel on my brake to slow our progress so they can catch up. It's a delicate balance; if I get too far ahead, her team might shut down, but if my dogs stop, they might not start again.

Marker to marker, playful Juliet and meek Reno perform double duty: they are leading my team and Mel's. It's our long-awaited moment of triumph: a brilliant performance woven from our frayed strands of defeat on the sea ice. Juliet bounds ahead, her head down and her tiny shoulders as big as they can be. She's downhill from Reno; his tail blows across her back. Behind them in swing, Kanga and Spur push into the gale with a dedication impossible to ignore.

My sled acts like a sail: when the quartering wind makes it slip off course, the dogs compensate by pulling uphill. We're a determined team, strong enough to help another. Traversing that pass in front of Mel feels like many more miles than it actually is.

Mel and I run together for the next three days—to the checkpoint of Iditarod and on to Shageluk. Those snow-laden trail miles are punchy and riddled with deep holes; progress is slow. Our bodies get thrashed as we tip into one crater after another. Just when we think we can take no more we reach an open creek. We wade up to our waists in winter water and coordinate pulling both teams across. When Zeppy tangles with Taiga, Mel pulls them to safety. Mel's team is swimming when her head lamp burns out. Quickly I hand her my spare.

We spend two nights camping: one in a moldy cabin infested with mice, another in our sleds during a miserable thirty-degree rainstorm. During these stops we exchange stories; we joke about spending more time facedown in the snow than standing on the runners. We take off our hats and compare our haven't-showered-for-a-week hair. Mel and I squat next to each other and pee in the snow as if we're two puppies. We complain that the precooked meals we've sent out on the trail have spoiled from the warm weather, and we dutifully dine on energy bars and freeze-dried beef stew that resembles salted cardboard. We fantasize about fine wine while gulping warm energy drinks out of thermoses one week grungy.

Later I'm told by an official that word traveled down the trail that two tiny women with long strings of dogs knew how to have fun.

"No one enjoyed Iditarod more than you did," he said.

It is true that Mel and I thrive in each other's company and so do our dogs—and the lessons don't stop there. I learn that my habitual independent manner does not necessarily enlighten a journey, and that pairing up with another means more than doubling the numbers. To realize that my backyard dog team can keep pace with hers is an honor. I am heartened beyond measure that the dogs from my 2003 scratch have enough drive to share.

As much as I don't want to, when we've been in Shageluk for more than eight hours, I elect to leave before Mel. She's pulling her clothes out of the village dryer when we say good-bye. She tells me she has no choice but to give her yearlings an extended rest there. Knowing that my own team needs to keep moving on a consistent schedule, I decide to keep to my plan. We talk about adjusting a future rest stop so we can run together again, but we know that might not be realistic. As my dogs speed away, I look over my shoulder at her team resting. A true traveling companion is hard to come by. I hope I'm not making a big mistake.

The run from Shageluk to Anvik is short: twenty-five miles. We stop long enough to sign in and out at 9:30 PM. When we leave the village, I recognize the wide, sweeping turn. This is where Kanga guided us over the black ice in 2003.

Everything is different now. In contrast to 2003, we will follow the Yukon for a relatively short 250 miles. As we cruise in moonlight bright enough to cast shadows of dogs on the snow, I'm pleased to be on the river. At last I can hold the handlebars lightly and give my swollen fingers a rest. Maybe my shoulders will heal. Perhaps the Yukon will be kind.

As I so often do, I focus the beam of my head lamp on each individual husky. There are thirteen now. I dropped big, fuzzy Wolf in Iditarod for a slightly sore hip. Everyone else is healthy and sound. The seven who ran in 2003 are still here: Juliet, Sydney, Taiga, Spot, Roulette, Strider, and Kanga.

Kanga. She's the one I cannot understand.

I study her smooth gait, her compact and perfect body, her subtle drive—and I think back to her spectacular performance over these exact miles two years earlier. Other than that last mile into Unalakleet, Kanga has refused to run up front ever since. This makes no sense for a dog with so much talent.

Now the smooth snowy trail is promising, so I take a chance. After hooking my sled to a driftwood log, I walk up to Kanga, praise her, and clip her in lead alongside Sydney. These are her miles of glory. I can't resist giving her one more try.

When I whisper, "Hike," the two leaders leap ahead. For a moment they're the epitome of grace: Sydney's easy rhythm alongside Kanga's smooth trot. I hold my breath and admire their erect ears, their easy, confident gaits that lend optimism to us all. But then it happens. Kanga slows and floats back alongside Reno. She noses her son before looking back at me with a split-second warning that she's about to sit down.

Don't ever run her in lead. Do everything to keep her happy.

Haunted by my own intentions, I stop the team quickly. This experiment could be way too costly. I put Kanga next to Zeppy in wheel. Instantly she yaps and jerks against the line, crazy to go. With Juliet up front alongside Sydney, I say, "Okay."

All thirteen resume their spunky Iditarod trot.

Now soothed by the tonic of momentum, I sip ginger mint tea and contemplate how Kanga might have lost her spirit to lead. After a while we reach an intersection where the Iditarod Trail diverges from the well-worn village "highway" we've been traveling. Iditarod markers veer to the left and follow the shore.

"Haw, Sydney and Juliet. Haw!" I say.

They swing toward the markers but then back to the right, confused. Meanwhile Kanga barks and pulls hard to the left from wheel. My wisest leader—with all the talent yet no longer the heart—tries to take charge from the back of the line.

The run from Grayling to Eagle Island is long, but our progress is steady and sure. From the start of the race I've looked forward to being on the river, and now the wide, mellow expanse calms me. To navigate the well-traveled trail that connects the Yukon villages means I no longer have to worry about enduring the next turn. It's all about finding a comfortable traveling tempo and pausing every few hours to offer the dogs a snack.

In the heat of the day we pause for a brief rest in the sun. I wish Mel was here to nap alongside us, but I remind myself to focus on our own run-rest plan. The dogs are spunky when we get back under way, a good indication that we're running a cadence that will sustain us beyond Shaktoolik.

We pull into Eagle Island on a quiet, mild evening. There is no village here, just a few tents, long lines of straw where others have rested, and a pile of half-empty drop bags. A plane on skis is taking off as I arrive. I recognize it from other checkpoints, as part of the volunteer "Iditarod Air Force." A group of professional pilots volunteer for no payment other than fuel and food, in order to support Alaska's last great adventure. These tireless aviators ferry supplies and workers to the checkpoints and transport dropped dogs. I wave at the pilot as he flies over us and then notice a familiar figure running toward me.

"Zeppelin, you bad boy! How the hell did you get all the way out here?" Eric, a friend from Denali Park, welcomes us. His greeting takes me by surprise. Here on a remote bend of the Yukon River is a handler who worked in Zeppy's kennel when he was a pup. Evidently, the dog's reputation was established early on. When Eric spots him on Iditarod, he greets him like a first-grade teacher reconnecting with a trouble-maker from the past.

Eric and I are exchanging a few words about Zeppy when Jim Gallea, Andy and Hannah's Junior Iditarod friend, shows up. After running Iditarod several times, Jim's now a volunteer. He gives me a bear hug before showing us a camping spot and a fresh bale of straw. Delighted to be in the company of friends, I begin chores. Booties come off. Water boils in my cooker. A veterinarian checks the dogs and confirms that they're all in fine health.

Suddenly I have a sharp pain in my left side.

"Hey, Jim, you guys have bathroom facilities out here, right?" I ask.

"We built the sweetest loo you'll ever find," he replies, pointing to a blue-tarped outhouse one hundred yards away. "We made it just for you," he adds with a smile.

I've taken only three steps when a wave of nausea rolls through me. By the time I reach the "sweet" destination, I am fighting the urge to lose all that I have consumed, both ways at once. The urgency of my problem is complicated by many layers of clothing. I have to remove two jackets in order to take off my one-piece suit. Or I could unzip the crotch zipper of my suit and wrestle with two layers of flapped long underwear.

To manage these logistics in the confines of a blue-tarped outhouse the size of a phone booth, and its smelly bucket, is no easy or pleasant proposition. One step inside those wicked blue walls, and I am miserably ill. I fumble for zippers while fouling my pants; at the same time, I throw up in the snow. Wracked with nausea, I shiver, then lose more and more food—ultimately kneeling over the bucket, then sitting on its throne designed for rituals far less debilitating.

For a moment I'm better. But what to do next? My legs are a sticky, smelly mess. Anywhere else I'd be mortified, but I'm on a one-thousand-mile mission and must contend with one detail at a time. At that moment it makes perfect sense to take off all my pants, get back to the water warming in my cooker, and clean myself off. I'm pulling off my boots when I remember that there could be some clean long johns in my Eagle Island drop bag. Or did I send those to Kaltag? Either way, an emergency set is stowed in my sled.

In a matter of a minute I peel off my suit and my multiple pant layers. Then, without running water, I do my best to clean myself off. Next I put my boots back on. Bare-bottomed, wearing only two shirts and an anorak, I trudge toward my sled to regroup. I'm looking at my feet, convinced that if I don't look at anyone, they won't see me, when someone approaches. Then there's a voice.

"Debbie how was your . . . run?" Mel says, pausing midsentence and looking at me like I might have gone mad.

I explain what has happened and tell her that under no circumstances should she get into that outhouse. I don't remember how our conversation ends, but I do recall Jim walking up.

"Pretty nice accommodations, eh, Debbie?" he says. Evidently in the dusky light he doesn't see me clearly until he's at my side. Then he realizes that he's talking to a bare-legged musher who resembles a chicken wearing a blue parka.

"What the hell?" Jim doesn't know what to say.

"I am so sick," I reply. "Give me a second."

"Oh no!" He looks at me while backing up. "I'll check back with you later."

As he walks away, I throw up again into the snow. Then, fearing I'll only feel relief for a matter of minutes, I hustle back to my sled, where I use extra dog water to wash off my insulated pants, locate clean long underwear, and wrestle them on. With nausea rising, I feed the team before stumbling into a tent that's been set up for weary mushers. I crawl into my sleeping bag and shiver.

My race clock has stopped. There is no way I can leave the checkpoint until I'm able to hold down water. Too sick to be discouraged, I focus on the hope that this misery will pass. One more trip to the outhouse ends my series of gastrointestinal events. Then I'm in and out of woozy sleep, listening to teams coming and going.

"Debbie, can you go?" Mel taps me on the shoulder, hoping we'll run together to Kaltag. I know it would be safer to travel with her, but I can't leave. I haven't even tried drinking water.

"You better go on without me," I say.

Mel's not happy. "That's the worst!" she replies. She goes on to say words that I'm thinking. "I know you'll be better soon. You have to be." Then she adds a promise. "I'll wait for you up ahead—come as soon as you can. We'll travel the coast together."

The coast. Mel knows about my demons on the coast.

She pushes the tent flap closed, and I roll over onto my cramped stomach. Mel has to do what's right for her dogs and move on, but to run in her company again would be a welcome lifeline. I listen to her team barking and hear her ask them to go. As I slip into a sticky, uncomfortable sleep, I'm determined to catch up with her soon.

Cool air seeps through the seams in the tent walls and wakes me. My watch reads 7:30 AM. I've slept on and off for nearly eight hours. I'm no longer nauseous, and I know it's important to get up and drink. It isn't cold—maybe twenty degrees—so calories from food aren't critical, but hydration matters.

Jim meets me at the door of the tent and asks how I'm feeling. I tell him better, that I plan to feed the team and get ready to leave. After tea and pilot biscuits, I plan to take off before noon. He gives me some antidiarrhea medicine, the same kind we give the dogs. I will myself through chores.

My huskies are well rested and happy. They eagerly gobble their food. I repack the sled and slowly prepare to depart. My head pounds, but my stomach is calm. At 11:00 AM we go.

The team is raring to run, and I let them move a little faster along the miles where Lil' Su guided us through the nighttime storm.

God, I miss you, Lil' Su.

At least the weather is quiet and the temperatures mild.

Within a few hours my throat is raw with pain and my head is stuffed with congestion. What began in my gut turns into the respiratory flu. By the time we run up the ramp to Kaltag, I'm hacking with a deep, raspy cough.

Unlike their musher, my dogs are full of spunk. Sydney, Juliet, and the others scamper up the bank from the river and onto the village lane lined with children. I sign in with the checker, who has received a message that I'm ill.

"You okay, Debbie?" he asks.

"Just fine," I reply. "I'll stay for a good eight-hour rest, then move on. Has Mel taken off?" I ask.

"Just a few moments ago," he answers. "She said to tell you she'll see you in Unalakleet."

Juliet in her sleeping bag

25

Dog Time

I check into Unalakleet with thirteen dogs at 8:28 PM on Wednesday, March 16. Those are the facts, but when I set my snow hook into the ice of the Unalakleet River, I have no clue what day of the week it is. The calendar means nothing. Instead, hours and minutes are defined by my huskies. It's all about running and resting. After a long rest at Old Woman, we ran to Unalakleet. We'll stop here for eight hours and then travel on to Shaktoolik. We're living in dog time, moving down the trail.

I do have a plan, one that has everything to do with the cycle of day and night. The sun has recently set, and I want to be under way again before it rises. That way we'll be on a perfect schedule. We'll go over the Blueberry Hills in daylight and rest in Shaktoolik during the bright afternoon. Then, as the sun slips behind the horizon, my dogs and I will move again. This time they'll run past the snow fence in the cool, dusky light that intrigues them.

We'll run right past the shelter cabin.

We will cross Norton Sound in darkness. In the black of night, they won't have to confront the endless white ice. They might not realize they've been there before.

If all goes well, we will pull into Koyuk a little before midnight. Regardless of the calendar, our arrival will herald the beginning of a new day; we'll be looking at miles of the Iditarod Trail we've never traveled before.

The trudge up the bluff toward the Unalakleet checkpoint is long. I'm thinking about my drop bags, trying to remember if I sent chicken and rice here or the less appealing beef stroganoff, when a small figure bounces toward me.

"Hey, girl. I knew you'd catch us! I'm so happy to see you!"

It's Mel. Because we checked in after dark, I hadn't seen her dog team sleeping. I figured she had long ago moved on. Mel is all rested and cheerful. She tells me to get some sleep and adds, "I'm going to wait for you. We'll run the coast together."

I cannot believe that in the midst of her own Iditarod battle she is willing to make plans around mine. I tell her my team needs to rest until 5:00 AM. That works for her; she's pleased to double her own sleep.

Within an hour we're stretched out side by side on the sticky floor of the Unalakleet bingo hall. Mel is snoring and I'm wide awake. My cough is irritating, but my mind is the real distraction. I'm recalling the 2003 run to Shaktoolik. The icy sidehills, the cliff in the night. The harsh sting of the wind. Somewhere in the shadows between awake and asleep, Kanga glowers alongside a broken door. I beg her to be happy and then plead with the rest. I can't understand what's gone wrong.

When the alarm rings at 3:00 AM, Mel groans. I'm relieved. It's time to run to Shaktoolik. Time, at last, to move on.

Mel's team goes first, and we follow close behind. We pass the slough that was mirrored ice in 2003, and this time it's covered with snow. The nasty pitches are nothing in daylight. I wonder if these miles are as tough as I remember, or if the memory of them is the problem—a burden to ignore.

While Mel and I climb into the hills, I study each dog. Everyone looks good. Running strong. This is what we've worked for: to arrive at the coast steady and focused.

One minute I'm admiring my impressive thirteen dogs, and the next, as if needing something to fret about, I notice their hipbones. Fang and Snickers and Spot are my best eaters; they look okay, but I'm convinced that the others are too thin. The vet back in Unalakleet assured me that they're fine, explaining that it's typical for huskies to drop weight during a marathon, but now I remember a dream: Denny, the Shaktoolik vet, is examining the team and telling me I have to scratch because the dogs are dangerously thin. Maybe the other vet was wrong.

The nightmare taunts me with a devastating possibility: Sydney and Juliet are picky eaters, and during the race they've dropped more weight than the rest. *What if they can't go on?*

I'm spinning a web of worry when Mel motions me past. It's my turn to go out front. I call up the dogs and swing around her, and the trail reclaims my focus.

We pass short, scrubby trees and thickets of willows. Lacy patterns in the snow left from ptarmigan scurrying. Tracks of a fox dragging its tail. A steep uphill grade means I have to get off the sled and run. It's really more of a fast walk, which is all I can muster. I'm hacking away when we crest the mountain and pitch over the top. We're surging once more down the sweeping descent to the sea.

Somewhere on the exhilarating ride, I spot Shaktoolik in the distance. There's a cluster of buildings on a narrow spit of land. I can actually see open water—dark blue to the west. Everything else is white.

There it is: the WELCOME TO SHAKTOOLIK banner rapping against the familiar checkpoint building. The door opens, and here come the volunteers. Denny reaches me first and wraps her arms around me.

"Hey, Debbie! Here you are again! Good for you!"

She's uncharacteristically jolly. In my growing state of insecurity, I figure she's trying to pump me up. Denny leads me around to the lee of the building, where she lines out my dog team alongside a few others. As I dole out straw, I'm telling her about my dream. Even while the words spill out, I'm embarrassed—these are things to think and not say, but I'm too tired to hold them in.

"Oh, Denny, I'm so scared you'll pull us out of the race," I tell her.

"Well, if they're too thin, that's exactly what I'll do," she responds in her typical straightforward manner.

Denny's words rumble through me, but I continue to hand out salmon snacks. I'm nervously nudging straw into perfect mounds with my boots when Mel pulls in. She talks with Denny while a different vet introduces himself to me and examines my team.

I stumble around in an anxious shuffle, keeping busy with my drop bags while the vet goes dog to dog. When the examination is complete, he puts the stethoscope inside his parka—and my heart pounds.

"Debbie, I have to tell you," he says, looking me in the eye. "They're beautiful. This is one of the best-looking teams that's come through here."

I've finished feeding and massaging the dogs when my friend and fellow 2003 musher Palmer Sagoonik walks up. He isn't running Iditarod this year; instead he's helping out at his hometown checkpoint.

"Debbie, how are you? Welcome back to Shaktoolik."

He gives me a hug. Looking at his weathered face and animated dark eyes reminds me of the day during the 2003 race when he passed me after I'd fallen asleep on the Yukon. He teased me then, and his sense of humor perked me up. Now he has something different to say.

He puts his hands on my shoulders and looks me in the eye. "You're going to get to Koyuk this time. You believe that, right?"

I nod. Then he turns his gaze to the sea. "So, Debbie, you know we're on a narrow spit here. Right? Did you see the open water to the west just now when you ran in? This year the sea never froze over there. Crazy warm winter."

He scans the landscape with reverence.

"You listen to me, Debbie. You throw your doubts over there in that water. You understand. Just *dump* them in that water." He takes a step back and, as if he's throwing a ball, tosses something imaginary toward the west.

Then he continues, "Now. Look to the east; there is ice. You go out there and take with you strong faith that you and your dogs will make it. I've been out there many times this week, praying for you on that ice. You'll do fine, but you have to believe."

There's no way for me to respond. This wisdom comes from a man who understands this place as well as his own heart. I thank him, and then he delivers one more gift. He tells me that after I'm done feeding dogs, I should come in to eat. His wife has just brought over some of her best caribou stew.

Mel and I rest six hours, and we leave Shaktoolik shortly after 6:00 PM. Sydney and Juliet are in lead, with Reno and Spur behind. Next are Fang and Snickers, Zeppy and Topaz. These are the eight who were not with me on the ice in 2003. Those who were—Taiga, Roulette, Strider, Spot, and Kanga—are all positioned near the sled, at the back of the line. Kanga is running wheel alongside ever-earnest Spot. She's close to the sled so that I can watch her; if she begins to balk from wheel, she shouldn't influence the others.

Mel tells me to go first. She's worried her young dogs don't have enough confidence for the crossing. I don't question her request. Instead I tell myself that the wind is light and the temperatures mild. Darkness is coming. This is the perfect time of day for the crossing.

We'll reach the other side.

When I call, the dogs leap to their feet. Someone leads them around the building and across the street and then sets us free. The team scrambles down the berm, and we pass driftwood and markers that have been knocked to the ground. Then the dreaded snow fence.

Before we reach it I'm reliving the sequence from 2003. The incessant *rat tat tat tat* of the barricade flapping in the wind. Kanga's hesitation. Lil' Su looking back. Taiga's flat ears.

Today the fence beckons, and Juliet and Sydney run past it.

In another hundred yards we're near the place where our trouble began. Spot pulls to the side. He wants to pee. I notice the telltale yellow marks on the trail where others have marked their passage, so his impulse makes sense. Of course Spot and the rest need to add their signatures, so I call the team to a stop. When I ask them to go again, they're eager. Kanga looks over her shoulder at me.

"Straight ahead, Kanga!" I snarl.

She lowers her head and drives forward. I apologize for being a little jumpy.

We've been running for an hour when the sun vanishes, and the white landscape shifts from tones of pink to lavender to gray. In the dusky light we near Island Point, where the shelter cabin stood. Palmer told me that high water had actually moved the cabin. Sure enough, I see its dilapidated form on the ice ahead. Markers lead us alongside it.

"On by!" I shout. Then again, "On by!"

I call encouragement to the dogs as we pass the shack's crooked frame, its cracked windows and splintered walls. I sneer at its nervy relocation so close to our trail. The dogs accelerate, and we leave the damned shack behind.

We are rolling.

Darkness deepens. My head lamp illuminates ice and trail markers that gleam in the night. I'm surprised that the surface here isn't flat, and then I wonder if the undulating seascape is the result of my weary imagination. No. There are real hollows and gentle rises. Great fracture lines, stripes of snowdrifts, and areas with no snow at all. This place isn't featureless—it's alive, a frozen topography that makes me edgy and alert. That's why I don't miss it when Juliet first floats back. I call encouragement to her, and she leaps ahead for a few strides and does it again.

"No, no, Juliet. No!"

Then I tell her she's beautiful, but she looks back at me with anxious eyes. She looks stressed, so I hustle to switch her with Reno. He's happy to go, but within a short time he and Sydney begin to weave from left to right, like they're disoriented. Mel's team is running close behind us, so I blink my light at her twice, signaling that we need to talk.

When she walks to my sled I ask her to pass, explaining that I'm unsure if I have a problem but don't want to take any chances. Her dogs are willing to go by, and mine tuck in at a nice pace behind them. Now Reno and Sydney are eager—they'd rather follow than lead. Kanga runs steady in wheel, and I don't dare say one word. For the next hour, I silently will Mel's team onward.

Neither my dogs nor Mel's are their usual selves that night. At times they act confused and veer off the marked trail. Sometimes they slow to a walk. Perhaps they're spooked by the sea. Or maybe Mel and I are unsettled, and our huskies sense our discomfort. Either way, brake marks etched in the ice reassure that others have been here before us. And the distant shifting lights of Koyuk coax us forward.

It's nearing midnight when everything changes. We pass boulders of ice, and Mel's team zigs and zags. Suddenly there's a tuft of grass under my runners. We're off the ice. Then we're not, but land must be near. Finally the dogs scramble up a hillside of dirt. Within a few minutes, we're beneath the village lights of Koyuk.

This is no ordinary checkpoint arrival. I usually focus on chores in order to stay on schedule. For the first time in the race, I haven't even considered the next run. Maybe I'm superstitious, or perhaps I know better than to assume success. For whatever reason, it's always been "if" we reach Koyuk rather than "when."

Now that we're here, it's all about praising tail-wagging dogs and wiping frost off whiskers. Tossing celebratory snacks of salmon and herring, beef and lamb. Rubbing Taiga's belly and asking Spot to sing. A handful of teams are parked along the village lane. Smiling around us are villagers and checkpoint volunteers, including Caroline the vet, Dianne the checker, and a Koyuk family dressed in colorful parkas trimmed with fur. Someone hands me a note of congratulations—a message called in from Denny and the crew in Shaktoolik. Al, the race judge who knows our family from Junior Iditarod, tells me, "Good job."

These well-wishers make me happy, but I'm thinking of Mark and Andy and Hannah. How they'll shout with relief and raise a glass when they know that we're in Koyuk. I've hardly called them during this race; more than anything, I want to talk to them now. But I know that tonight they don't need to hear my voice to know that I'm happy. I bet we have made them proud.

Mel and I are in high spirits the next morning when we prepare to leave Koyuk. With the Norton Sound crossing behind us, we're elated to share the final miles of the race. We've even talked about the real calendar, and discovered that it's Friday, March 18. This is important because the Iditarod Finishers' banquet takes place on Sunday night. We know we will get there in time. We'll run the final miles of Iditarod together. Our teams are healthy, big in dog numbers, and strong. Together we've designed a run-rest plan for the coast that will result in a Saturday finish. If bad weather holds us up, there is an entire day to spare.

Surrounded by a cluster of onlookers, I cinch the straps on my sled bag. Then I check with Mel to make sure she's ready. She gives me a thumbs-up. We've agreed it's my turn to lead.

I thank everyone and call, "Ready!" All thirteen leap to their feet. Spot woofs, and so does Taiga. Zeppy chews his neck line.

"See you in Nome!" someone shouts.

"Oh yes, you will!" I respond.

I glance at Mel, and we exchange smiles. Then my spunky huskies and I charge away from the crowd. Elim is forty short miles away.

A grassy, windblown bluff comes first, and then a short descent to the sea. We zip onto the ice and follow markers that lead across a bay. I'm admiring the coastline—the view of high bluffs and a rocky cliff called Moses Point—and am not paying attention when the dogs bunch up. The sled swings to an awkward halt, and I figure they must have to pee—this far into the race it's common, soon after leaving a checkpoint, for one male to stop, prompting the others to relieve themselves in unison. I give them a moment and then ask them to go. They move a few steps, and then every single dog sits down.

"Reno! Spur! What are you thinking?" I walk along the line and ruffle everyone's fur, then get back onto the runners. "Let's go!" I call. "Hike, hike, hike!"

No one moves.

I look for a tangle, or for one dog who's uncomfortable. Of course there must be a simple explanation for a slowdown that could be readily fixed. But at the same time a familiar dread creeps through me. I feel weightless running up to the leaders to switch Reno and Spur with Sydney and Juliet.

"Stand up, stand up!" I cry.

I'm ready to pull the hook when Mel passes, raising her arms in confusion. I wave her by, praying Juliet and Sydney will follow. Mel's team bounds ahead. Mine watches with disinterest.

Mel keeps going, and I rush once more to my leaders, this time to try Fang with Sydney. As I hustle back to the sled, I scold Kanga, who's sitting. I pick her up and put her on her four feet. "You stand, got it?

Stand!" Then I notice Roulette and Strider sulking. I ask the team to go, and no one responds.

When I stand still on the ice and look at my team, conflicting advice from 2003 weaves through my mind. One Iditarod champion put it this way: "Debbie, at the first balk you should have gone back to the checkpoint and dropped any dog who might have caused it. After a meal and a rest, you could have had a fresh start."

Another disagreed. "Never go back to a checkpoint. Ever. Don't let the dogs get their way," he said.

It's never the dogs' fault.

This is my philosophy.

In the midst of debating my next move, I notice motion on the ice: a dog team heads toward us from Elim. At first I think my eyes are tricking me, but they aren't: it's Mel. Somehow she must have turned her team around. Within a few minutes her long line of dogs faces mine. Our leaders stand nose-to-nose. Mel and I meet in the middle.

"Oh, Debbie. Just look at them! My God, what's happened?" She articulates my own dismay.

"Who knows?" I answer. "You know how happy they were when we left." What I'm really thinking is that I'm so grateful for a witness—for someone else to see this unimaginable canine mood swing.

"I've never seen anything like it," she continues. "Do you mind if I talk to them?"

"Not at all," I reply, hoping that negative feedback from Mel might make them reconsider.

She walks down my line, speaking to each pair. "Juliet, no, you stand up. Roulette, what are you thinking?" On she goes: "Bad girl, Kanga. You stand."

Her rounds complete, she talks to me, as if I'm the next dog on the line. "So I'm going to run past you back toward Koyuk, turn my guys around, and pass you from behind. You get on them and get them to chase, okay?"

I thank her and say I'll do all that I can. Then I tell her to keep going if we don't follow—that this behavior can be contagious.

"Don't let us wreck your run," I say.

Mel completes the head-on pass, then I watch her direct her team into a running 180-degree turn. To do such a thing, so close to the Koyuk checkpoint, is both impressive and risky. Once they are turned, she stops to deliver praise. Then they run toward us from behind.

As they near, I'm yelling, "Woohoo! We're going to go! Let's go, let's go!"

Not one dog shows a hint of interest. When Mel's team runs by us, my dogs are sitting on the ice, glowering. She turns to look back and shakes her head. As my friend disappears into the white haze, it occurs to me that she's moving along a trail we may never travel.

I stand alongside my dogs, and everything is quiet. It's that profound stillness that arrives in a flash, when everything changes. Like the moment nurse Ruby called to say Mom would soon die. Or when I was wedged inside the crevasse: something had ended and there was also a beginning, but I could not tell one from the other.

Right now we are not moving. Mel's team has run out of sight, and we are stuck on the sea ice. I am stunned, yet I know that in time momentum will come. Deep within me lives hope for a new chance. I just have to find it.

I walk to my leaders. Without saying a word, I turn my thirteen-dog team and point them back toward Koyuk. When I step onto the runners, my huskies stand tall, their ears high. My rebellious dogs have plenty of energy to lope off the ice and up the bluff, back to the check-point.

Topaz

26

Resolve

Everything about Koyuk is different when I return. A team has just arrived, and I don't recognize the musher. Villagers who watch me dole out straw talk in hushed voices. Despite the warming sun, the morning feels damp and dark.

I'm getting the dogs settled when Al the judge walks up. He's looking down at his feet, like he wishes he didn't have to see me.

"Uh . . . Debbie," he says. "You here to cancel?"

Cancel?

He has got to be kidding. Al's awkward suggestion that I might pull out of the race only intensifies my resolve. I tell him that I have no intention of scratching, that I'm back in Koyuk to drop some dogs, and that we'll leave again when there's a team to follow.

"All right," he says, and walks away.

I'm sitting on my sled, trying to decide which dogs need to fly home, when Caroline walks up. She looks at me with a warm smile and tells me she's sorry. "Kanga's too dangerous to run on the coast, isn't she?" she says.

Caroline is one of the finest Iditarod veterinarians; she's familiar with my dogs and their individual racing histories. I tell her she's right and that sadly there are two others. Roulette and Strider have been sour for several days—they should have gone home a while ago.

"What about Taiga?" Caroline asks. "She was also with you in 2003, right?" Taiga is sleeping—her chin on the snow between outstretched paws—looking completely put out. I respond that despite her body language, Taiga is actually pretty happy; she's also a valuable backup leader. Caroline advises me to fill out dropped-dog paperwork for Taiga just in case.

"That way when you ask them to leave, if she doesn't look willing, I can take her quickly."

I have to admit, this is a generous offer.

When Caroline comes with leashes to take my three dogs, I explain that I'll walk Kanga to the dropped-dog tent myself. She could well be the "one" who is causing our troubles, but it pains me to leave her behind.

Kneeling alongside her, I unclip Kanga from the line. Then I linger with her for a moment. Kanga's my master veteran who has mentored the rest. Her leading skills were brilliant in Wyoming; her dedication up front unmatched. This is my lead dog who sits on the couch and rides in the cab of the truck. She posed in my lap for my first Iditarod musher card. How can it be that this dog has twice been part of my race's unraveling?

As I stroke her face, I do see trouble. There is no denying that Kanga's alpha streak rules our dog yard. She's understated, but one intense, moody girl. Today she was positioned in the middle of the line. It never occurred to me that anything could go wrong, so I wasn't even watching her. Now I stand and walk my muscled, healthy leader to a line of dropped dogs. Before leaving her I sit on the straw and rest my cheek against hers. I tell her I'm sorry. I don't know exactly what has happened, but I consider this failure my own.

When I return to my gang of ten, I notice the musher who's parked next to us. He looks like he might be twenty years old. He wears his neck gaiter on his head, which reminds me of the Cat in the Hat. Someone, either Caroline or Al, introduces us. His name is Andrew, and when I ask if we might follow him out of the checkpoint, he's agreeable. He says he'll head out around 2:00 PM. I tell him we can go anytime; it's not like my dogs need more rest. I feel so inept, relying on another musher, but the plan makes good sense.

At 1:55 PM Andrew's team stands. I ask my dogs to do the same. They do, all except Taiga. She remains curled up on the snow, so I nod to Caroline, who takes her. It has to be done.

When Andrew leaves, Sydney and Reno are happy to follow. With tall ears and bright eyes, all nine run with frisky curiosity about the team ahead. I hold my breath as we motor past the place where they balked only a few hours earlier. Eager to chase, now they move well on the ice. It's like they don't even remember. Like nothing ever went wrong.

It takes me a good half hour to trust this reversal of fortune. By that time Sydney and Reno are charging, wanting to pass Andrew, but I don't let them. Instead I ride my drag with both feet, not caring one bit about speed. We could walk to Nome; any movement is better than none. That their spirit is back makes me happiest of all.

As we settle into a controlled slower pace, I praise each dog by name: Sydney and Reno, Spur and Juliet, Zeppy, Fang and Topaz, Snickers and Spot.

The team is so small, it doesn't seem right. So I name the others: "Kanga. Roulette. Strider."

Taiga. I never said good-bye.

Lightning. Wolf. Lil' Su—what if you were here?

Now that we're moving, I can't stop wondering what has happened. I revisit that endless debate, the unsolvable riddle: what went wrong in 2003, and what has made them balk again? These dogs love to go. From the moment we put them in harness as pups, through countless races and thousands of training miles, they have lived for the trail. I'm the weak link, clinging to the handlebars for a wild ride.

After my scratch I asked friends for advice. Many theorized that the dogs knew me better than I knew myself, and that from my own weary psyche I must have passed an inner negativity to them. One musher told me that I must be scared of the coast—but I'm not. Our dogs mirror our selves. That fact is undeniable, but this morning's balk disproves the theory that I have some hidden phobia. When we left Koyuk, I was elated, pumped with confidence. So were my huskies.

What is it about the sea ice?

This familiar question has no easy answer, so now I consider the huge quantity of kibble I'm feeding and wonder if this is all about diet. Could this behavior be the result of a simple metabolic slowdown? Am I feeding too much? The possibilities circle in my mind, and I vow to let them go. There's no point in chasing my tail.

Most of an hour goes by. And like my dog team, I am antsy to pass Andrew. We're still on the ice, but I can't wait any longer. It's not like me to hold them back when they're this happy, so I give them the go-ahead.

"Okay, Reno and Sydney. On by!" We accelerate past. I shout thanks to Andrew and his funny hat. Soon he's a dot on the ice, far behind us.

The dogs surge up a steep hill into the village of Elim as if we've been on a ten-mile training run. When we pull up to the fire hall that serves as the checkpoint building, we're welcomed by a swarm of playful children and a checker who has heard about our sit-on-the-ice trouble.

"You'll do fine, Debbie," he tells me. "Your dogs look strong. You just need to be tougher on them." There it is: one more man who understands nothing about me or my huskies, but he *knows* that I'm too easy on them. I don't respond.

"So how long will you stay?" he asks.

"Will you sign my notebook?" a little girl interrupts.

"Of course I will," I tell her, which prompts another child to tell me all about his pet dog. I listen to their breathless chatter, attempting to be friendly to the children while formulating my response to the judge.

"We'll leave one hour before Andrew," I tell him, knowing full well that I'm not answering his question—particularly since Andrew hasn't arrived yet. But there are three miles of sea ice outside of Elim, and it's important that Andrew will be coming along close behind us in case we have trouble. I've shifted into a new focus, one that will consume me until the end. No one, including the race judges, will tell me how to play out the last miles of this journey. The strategy is my own.

Andrew plans to leave at 1:00 AM, so we take off at midnight. Reno and Juliet trot along the village street and dart into a sharp right turn that takes us down to the bay. We've started across the sea ice, and I'm calling, "Good dogs!" when they all sit down.

Again.

This time I'm ready with a new trick. I walk up to the leaders with an extra line, clip one end to the gang line and the other around my waist. By being the third leader, I'll prove to the dogs that I am one of them.

They don't see it that way. As soon as I say, "Hike," Sydney lurches to the side and pretends she doesn't know me. Juliet plunks herself down, ears drooping, and glares. I take the hint—it's not particularly subtle—and lie down on top of my sled to wait for Andrew.

Within an hour Spot woofs. Sure enough there's a light bobbing behind us. Quickly I rouse the rest. When Andrew runs by us, Zeppy, Spot, and Fang jump onto their feet. But the others are not inspired. Andrew is gracious enough to coax them for a while, and they tentatively follow. After about ten minutes his encouragement convinces Sydney and Juliet to move like they mean it. Then Spur looks better. Fang and Zeppy engage. Within twenty minutes their engines are warm, and my dogs reach cruising tempo. Then my nervy little bunch wants to pass.

This time I won't let them. Until we're off the ice, nothing can convince me otherwise. Once we're running in the trees, I tell them, "Okay!" Again we leave Andrew behind.

For the second time in twenty-four hours my Iditarod dream is brought back to life. My huskies move beautifully when they want to. Now they power up the forested foothills of a peak called Little McKinley. The checker at Elim told me to expect strong winds on the one-thousand-foot-high summit. Sure enough, we're climbing through a thinning forest, nearing tree line, when I notice that high-pitched coastal whistle. Then there are a few flakes spinning. Within minutes we're engulfed in a raging blizzard.

Once again the terms of my challenge change. This is no longer about finishing a dog race. Instead we engage in the high-stakes game of navigating one more Bering Sea storm. To continue moving is our fundamental mission.

The upper half of Little McKinley is above tree line, completely exposed to arctic weather. This is the place where a professional Iditarod musher got separated from his team in a blizzard and nearly perished. Unable to crawl into his sled for shelter, he wandered for a long night without food or drink. When the storm lifted, his dogs were sleeping unharmed, ten feet away.

I'm recalling that well-known story while we push up the mountain. Gripping my handlebars as if my sled is life itself, I am immersed in a heart-pounding effort to lighten the dogs' load. Their heads are low, their bodies leaning into their harnesses. This would be a logical place for discouragement, but the team moves with force. Sometimes I see them all, and at other times I see only snowflakes billowing. Always there's momentum, however slow.

These dogs love a wicked challenge.

We must be near the summit when I realize we haven't passed a marker for a while. The thought of being off trail here is terrifying. I'm unfamiliar with this terrain; the possibility of cliffs comes to my mind. Yet for safety I know we have to keep moving.

"Good dogs!" I scream, while concentrating on keeping the sled upright. If we pause for an instant, my huskies might give in to the instinct to bed down. But they don't. These dogs who balk in lovely weather perservere up Little McKinley in an all-out blizzard. Juliet and Sydney bust through one drift after another for at least an hour. They might sit on the sea ice in sunshine, but in a storm they push up a mountain like a freight train.

Eventually the trail levels. I don't trust the sensation at first, but it becomes undeniable: we begin to glide downhill. With the welcome momentum comes a stab of worry: we're off trail. Still encased in billows of snow, I cannot see where we're going.

My fear about upcoming terrain turns out to be unfounded. As quickly as the storm sucked us in, it sets us free. The clouds are high and the lights of Golovin sparkle on a vast landscape below us. We might have gotten off course, but now it's easy to head in the right direction along a windblown gentle slope. I notice a light moving steadily away from the village, across a dark expanse. It must be Andrew—he evidently passed us in the storm. Now he and his dogs glide steadily across the wide expanse of Golovin Bay.

I don't yet know, as we're nearing Golovin, that the village is almost empty. I find out later that most locals had left for a weekend basketball tournament in a nearby village. When we reach the lit streets I'm surprised there's no sign of life. No smoke rising from a chimney, not one snow machine in sight. Granted, it's the middle of the night, but this is Iditarod. There has to be someone around.

"Straight ahead," I call as we trot along an icy lane and pass too close to a chain link fence. Swing dogs Spur and Fang get tangled, so I stop, pull the line wide, and ask the team to move onto the ice.

Surely Juliet and Sydney are happy now that the weather has calmed. They must see the perfectly straight line of markers that lead across the twenty-mile bay.

"Good girls, good girls," I call, only to witness them weave off course.

Now I respond with a raspy growl: "Straight ahead!"

My two playful leaders who just pushed through the high-mountain storm with brilliance turn and look at me, and within a hundred yards they slow to a stop. Topaz and Spur curl up. Juliet plunks herself into a sitting harrumph. I close my eyes, not wanting to see any more. This game is getting old.

One more time I set my hook in the ice and walk toward the line. I intend to scold each dog like everyone wants me to, but when I reach wheelers Topaz and Spot and take in their blank stares, I can't. Instead, dog by dog, I stroke every wet head and tell each friend that we're twenty short miles from a mandatory eight-hour rest in White Mountain. That there is nothing to fear. When I reach Juliet and Sydney, I gather my two little leaders in my arms. We sit like that for a while. Then the familiar reality looms: we can't just stay here forever. If the dogs won't move ahead, we should return to shore. There has to be *someone* around.

It's something like 7:00 AM when the team trots back to the village. After parking in front of a house with a big covered porch, I walk up the steps and knock on the door. I'm hoping there's a phone I can use to call race marshal Mark Nordman and talk through my options. This time no one will speak to him for me.

When I knock tentatively, no one answers. So I take off my mittens and pound on the door. In a heavy silence that signifies rejection, I turn to leave and notice a bloodied moose head on the table by the door. Later I'm told that this is a common sight in the villages. Moose heads are saved after hunts for culinary delicacies such as the tongue and brain. At the time I only see dead eyes.

An hour or so passes, and I ask the dogs to go one more time. Now when they sit down on the edge of the bay I leave them alone to sleep. It's 8:00 AM. Is there really no one awake in Golovin?

I'm sitting on the steps of some sort of office building, watching my team snooze, when a snow machiner pulls up. Delighted to interact with another human, I explain our predicament. He is an Iditarod volunteer who knows Mark Nordman. Now this friendly villager invites me inside. He dials Iditarod headquarters in Nome, asks for the race marshal, and hands me the phone.

"Hi, Mark, can you hear me? It's Debbie," I say.

"Yeesss," he says, in that tone of guarded anticipation. "Where the hell are you?"

"The dogs are stopped here in Golovin," I tell him. "They're miserable. Scared, I guess, of the ice." I take a deep breath that tickles a spell of coughing. Then I add, "Don't tell me I'm being too soft. If one more person tells me that, I'm going to explode. That's not how we run. Being hard on them won't help anyway."

More words spill out. I explain to him that we've had a fabulous run and that the dogs don't know where they are. "If this is their finish line, it's good enough for me," I say, surprising even myself. It's like being on the phone suggests that I have an option to stop right here.

I say that I don't want to wreck a wonderful journey by arguing with my dog team. "Besides," I add, "I've thought a lot about that belt buckle. It really isn't very good-looking anyway."

First comes silence, then his breathless response. "Debbie, you listen to me. Do you understand?"

I feel like I've been sent to the principal's office.

"There is one finish line for Iditarod, and I am looking at it. Is that clear? Now, you be patient, get creative, use your head. You'll get here. Got it?"

"Yes," I rattle.

He replies, "Now give the phone back to my volunteer."

They talk for a while, and then I'm handed the phone so Mark can explain. Evidently a villager will leave for Nome within an hour. When he drives by on his snow machine maybe my dogs will follow. If not, Mark suggests I try something else. Mark ends the conversation with encouragement: "Debbie, you're close. You'll make it. Now go back out there. I'll see you under the arch."

The damned arch is one hundred miles away. Under normal circumstances we would be there in a day or two. There's no telling how long it might take us now.

Sometime in mid-morning a young kid zips up on his snow machine, and the dogs leap to their feet. He stops for a moment to say hi, then zooms ahead. My huskies surge in delighted pursuit. Within five minutes my newest hero looks over his shoulder. I give him a thumbs-up, and he speeds away.

That's all it takes: something ahead of us for five little minutes. Now we cruise across twenty miles of ice as if we do it every day. The dogs accelerate all the way to White Mountain, averaging a blistering Iditarod pace of ten miles per hour. We arrive at the checkpoint in an all-out lope.

The judge is Andy Anderson. I last saw him at Rainy Pass after surviving the Happy River Steps. He greets me with a chuckle. "I talked to Nordman, Debbie. Good job. If your dogs can run like that, there's no question you're going to make it."

Then he points to the far end of the checkpoint, to the outgoing trail. "See that team leaving? It's Mel. She says to tell you she'll see you under the arch. She also told me to say that she's certain you'll get there."

White Mountain checkpoint, 77 miles from Nome

27

Going Home

"Go ahead, it's really okay," the volunteer says.

He's trying to talk me into taking a shower, but for some reason I resist. Of course the idea is tempting. It's been fourteen days since I last bathed. My hair feels like plastic; it reminds me of troll hair. My cuticles are patched together with superglue, never mind my jagged fingernails. I've put on clean long underwear every few checkpoints, but that doesn't make up for my being something far worse than filthy.

To get clean has a fundamental appeal, but to shower in White Mountain actually scares me. Immersing myself beneath a stream of warm water might well seduce me into a different world—one with crisp cotton shirts and my favorite sunglasses. Chocolate-covered strawberries and hearty red wine. My dogs don't need that stuff, and neither do I. We've traveled almost one thousand miles. Seventy-seven remain between here and the burled arch. I'll save the shower for another day.

The bathroom with running water isn't the only distraction in White Mountain. People mill around; some are race fans who have flown in from the Lower 48. I recognize a few familiar faces from home.

One friend offers messages from my other life: "Your family isn't getting much sleep, Debbie." Another adds, "We had one hell of a windstorm in Anchorage last week." Then there's the spacious kitchen down the hall with a potluck of choices: lasagna, cheesecake, something Mexican. My stomach is still flippy, so it's best to play it safe with Top Ramen for one more meal.

The hospitality at White Mountain is generous, but I'm not ready for weather reports from Anchorage, cheese enchiladas, soapsuds, or family reports. The best I can do for Mark, Andy, and Hannah is to concentrate on getting to Nome. So I keep to myself and claim a sleeping corner in a half-lit room. When I lie down on the luxurious carpeted floor, my agitated thoughts surrender to sleep.

I wake disoriented. Someone else is stretched out on the floor alongside me, and there are footsteps nearby. Then everything comes back, in pieces.

We're in White Mountain. There's one run to go. I lurch forward with purpose. *I have to get to my dogs.*

I want to feed them a good meal and massage their shoulders. Sort out my gear and prepare to leave. Clutching my sleeping bag in one hand and the cooler full of warm water and thawed beef in the other, I trundle down the steep bluff. I might be groggy, but to reach my dog team is to find my way home.

They're snoozing so soundly it takes more than a casual greeting to wake them. Sydney raises her drowsy head, and Fang stretches, moans, and rubs his face in the cool snow. Zeppy looks sheepish. Sure enough, he's chewed his harness in two. No Iditarod dog destroys a harness this far into the race. At least I have one last spare.

At 5:00 PM I dish out their meal. Everyone eats well, and the sound of lapping brightens my mood. When the bowls are empty, every dog curls up in the straw for more sleep. I tend to logistics.

Our mandatory rest here is almost over. We can leave at 7:00 PM. This is our last run, and while I know better than to assume a finish, it's time to lighten our load. I don't need thirteen dishes for nine dogs or Kanga's special coat. I put them aside, along with twenty wrist wraps and the homemade shepherd's pie that might have gone bad. Two collars, three harnesses, and a half-eaten chocolate bar. I cram these extras into a send-home bag, then change batteries in my head lamp and count three sets of booties. At 6:30 PM it's time to wake up the dogs.

Preparing the team to leave means confronting our troubles. It was easier to concern myself with the mess in my sled than to look Spur or Sydney in the eye. Those two are in such a deep slumber that I leave them alone, but Reno wakes easily when I pat him. He'll lead tonight for sure. Juliet is in a tight ball, deep inside her sleeping bag. When I say her name, her tail thumps a few beats. That's a good sign. Zeppy's new harness lies in the snow near him; I'll put it on him at the very last second. Spot sits up for a minute, looks around, and curls up as if he's hit the snooze button. Snickers lies next to him, her nose tucked under her tail.

A crowd gathers around us just before 7:00 PM. Watching a musher launch onto her final run to Iditarod glory is popular with fans who have traveled to White Mountain. Villagers also come down to the river to send off teams. I'm well aware of the audience smiling when I lure Juliet out of her sleeping bag. She stretches, and I reward her rosy outlook with a herring. Then I bootie the team and cinch the straps tight on my sled, like I have so many times before.

When our eight-hour rest is officially over, a volunteer walks up with the sign-out clipboard. "You're free to go anytime, Debbie," he says.

Let's hope we can.

I walk to leaders Reno and Sydney and wake them. Then I continue down the line praising each dog and fluffing up fur. When I take my place on the runners, I thank the good volunteers, smile at the audience, and reach for my snow hook.

"Hike!" I call.

No one moves. I try to sound upbeat. "Good dogs! Need to wake up more?"

I go up the line and back to the sled, patting and encouraging with a confident ring in my voice. I'm trying to deliver the ultimate pep talk, but inside I'm resigned to another delay. Worst of all is how this must look to everyone watching—like I've been terrible to my dogs.

I ask them to go one more time. Again: nothing. It's as if I'm speaking a language they don't understand. Their backs sway, ears flatten, tails curl tight under their bellies. In hindsight their theatrics are impressive, but at the time their drama inflicts a deadening pain. Juliet gives me a sour glare, then she points her nose to the ground. Within a few breaths, they're all curled up on the snow. Like we're back at the shelter cabin and nothing has happened since.

No one watching us speaks, but their voices clang like bells in my mind: *She should get mad at them. She can't let them get away with this. Poor dogs must be tired. This is her second Iditarod try. Sad.*

I know one thing: we have to get away from White Mountain. We need to work this out on our own. I glance at Andy, the race judge, and mutter something about moving around the corner. Then I clip a leash onto the front of the line, and next to Reno and Sydney I walk the team away from the checkpoint. With the eyes of the crowd on my back, we move out of sight around the bend in the river.

Once we're alone, I let my huskies lie down. So do I, on top of my sled. This time I'm numb. I don't have a specific plan. There is no use in second-guessing these nine rebellious hearts, no point in projecting their next move. The bruising setbacks and stunning recoveries have tossed my spirits back and forth, up and down, to the point that I don't feel or think anything at all.

Yet somehow, in my quieted and dispirited state, I'm receptive to a whisper of hope. It's like the elusive promise of Mom's last cast or Dad's message when he stood on the porch waving. While I'm lying on top of my frozen sled bag on the Fish River at the end of my thirteenth Iditarod day, my huskies are curled nose-to-tail in front of me, I know we can't—and I won't—give up on Nome. I believe we'll get there. I just don't know how.

The buzz of a snow machine wakes me. I have no clue which direction it's traveling, but before rising to my feet, I'm calling up the dogs. "Ready, ready!"

All nine raise their heads to watch the "iron dog" speed past us toward Nome. Spot stands and Snickers looks perky, like a chase might be good fun. But Sydney doesn't buy it. Juliet looks at Reno, who rests his head on his paws again. They all go to sleep.

Within a half hour or so I hear ravens cawing. It's nearly dark, time for the birds to roost. They cackle and cluck, and from behind us they swoop over the team. This time leaders Sydney and Reno leap to attention. Spot barks and Snickers stands. I scramble onto the runners as the feathered beauties alight on the trail a few yards in front of us.

When they lift off, the dogs chase, all nine keying off their winged leaders. I'm awestruck by this mythological fate, until the ravens veer away from the trail and flap toward a distant bluff. Juliet continues prancing in swing, but Sydney's line loosens and Reno hangs his head. Spur and Topaz sit and the rest lie down. I return to my perch and slip into a resigned, groggy sleep.

Dogs are panting, must be running. Could this be, or am I dreaming?

God, this is one dark night.

Then a gruff male voice. "On by, on by! Whoa now." A musher stops his sled just ahead of Sydney and Reno. "Debbie, wake up. Let's get you going," he says.

"Who's there?" I ask. My voice is hoarse and my throat is burning dry. I'm stumbling around still half asleep, spewing words of apology and gratitude and "Yes, thank you, I'll do my best to quickly get them going."

The man tells me to take it easy, that there's no need to rush. "We're going home," he says. I'm thinking that he must have meant *Nome* instead of *home* when I tell him I would do anything to get there.

Then he says more: "You'll get there. My dogs know where we are. We live in Nome. They're running home."

My breathing quickens. Now he has my complete attention. "Who are you, really?" I ask. It's impossible to trust his good words. So I shine my light straight into his face, which makes him squint.

"I'm Greg. Greg Parvin. I know your husband. He and I are on a committee together. Don't worry, Debbie. We'll travel together tonight. Let me know when you're ready."

We'll travel together tonight. Let me know when you're ready.

Apparently he trains here; there's no reason to doubt that they *are* running home. If his dogs are familiar with the upcoming miles, which are notoriously tricky, that means we likely won't distract them. This is better than any solution I could imagine. A too perfect ending to a story that has grown very long. I replace Reno with Juliet. Greg calls up his team, and I do the same. After a few false starts there's a coordinated tug on my gang line. Ever so slowly we move down the trail.

Juliet and Sydney are willing to chase, and I let them run close to Greg's runners. We travel that way for several river miles and beyond, through twists and turns in a scrubby swamp. Every few minutes Greg glances back to make sure we're still with him. His team travels significantly more slowly than we do; he explains later that they're recovering from the stomach flu. They may not win any speed records, but their pace is a beautiful thing.

My dogs, in contrast, behave like a bunch of overtired school kids. They are willing to trot, but whenever Greg stops, they tangle. Sydney swings behind Reno and Spur. Juliet rolls on her back, then pounces to Sydney's defense, while I walk alongside them and tell them to line up. Sometimes it takes a few minutes to undo the knots they've tied. This gives Spur the chance to pull off a bootie, and I have to put another one on. I'm always rushing, fumbling around, apologizing to Greg, and worrying that any stop might tempt more trouble. Greg just smiles. He and his dogs patiently wait. Whenever I'm ready, we move again.

We've been under way for more than an hour when I figure I'm hallucinating; in the beam of my head lamp is a line of markers rising straight up to the heavens. Greg stops and explains that we're looking at the first of the Topkok Hills. For years I've heard about these hills, and that there are seven. But never have I imagined that they are so steep or high. Why didn't Mark or Andy tell me? If Sydney and Juliet refuse to run along a meandering river, what will they do on these gigantic rollers?

It turns out there's no reason to fret. My huskies lean into their harnesses and tackle the first hill, just like they ran up Little McKinley. Then the rascals are intent on passing Greg. It seems unfair to slow them on such steep terrain, so I stop them at the bottom of each valley while letting Greg's dogs work their way up. Then we charge up the ascent and catch him near the top, before descending, the dogs in a hearty scramble and both my feet on the drag. By the time we've conquered all seven hills, my nine dogs think they're invincible. With spirits high, they key off one another, my lavish praise, and the irresistible dare to outpace the team just ahead.

We've traveled thirty miles when we descend a hill and pull alongside a shelter cabin. "We'd better stop here and get ready for the Blowhole," Greg warns. "The next twelve miles will be nasty tonight. They're calling for ugly winds. If you want to snack, do it now. There's no stopping once we're on the beach."

The beach.

How could I have forgotten about this next section of trail? I've long heard about these exposed miles that run along the shore. With heightened anxiety, I throw the dogs some herring, cinch down their coats, my hood strings, and everything else I can think of.

Compared with me, Greg is relaxed. He encourages me to go inside and take a look at the cabin. He explains that the Nome Kennel Club has just fixed it up, but I'm in no mood for sight-seeing. While he's indoors signing the logbook, I change a few booties and talk up my leaders. At last Greg reappears. His dogs take off again, and mine follow. I'm relieved to get back under way.

Quickly the air comes alive. Great streaks of snow fly in the beam of my light, and dog coats flap. In a matter of minutes we're engulfed in a furious, bellowing wind.

The dogs power through it, tangling once in a while but moving ever forward. There are a few swirling gusts distinct from one another, but mostly we contend with a raging wall of cold air that pummels and wails in the night. Greg often looks back to check that we're still with him. Again I let Juliet and Sydney run inches from his sled. Knowing a shutdown would be unbearable, I yell encouragement until my voice no longer works. My huskies press on, as if they understand that the stakes are too high for shenanigans.

For two hours that feel like ten, the fierce wind commands my attention. Even my thoughts are silenced. I'm hardly aware that we're navigating the Bering Sea coastline—pushing through a hurricane-strength gale in utter darkness past a place called the Blowhole behind a stranger whose dogs know the way. The wind is the loudest I've known, screaming a cry of raw wildness. I'm not afraid and never wonder about our safety. Those questions will come later. At the time all I know is that we're moving. The dogs are doing fine. That's all that matters.

Then something changes. For an instant it's a little quieter. Then a gust doesn't whip as hard, doesn't deliver quite the sting. We're following Greg across something that looks like a bridge when he turns and shouts. For the first time in a few hours I can hear him.

"We're almost there, Debbie. Almost to Safety."

A face appears in a frosted window. Then the man shuffles outside. Holding his hood to his face, he speaks to Greg and comes over to me.

"Are you really Debbie?" he asks, handing me a pencil to sign in. When I confirm that truth, his weathered face erupts in a smile. "Man, are we ever happy to see you. It's been a long time since you checked out of White Mountain. You have one worried family in Nome."

My family.

I've not thought of them for hours. Now I ache for Mark, Andy, and Hannah. With a raspy voice, I ask him to call them quickly. He scurries inside, leaving me long enough to begin to recognize the terms of a new landscape.

We've reached the Safety checkpoint. There are twenty-two miles to the finish. If I have to walk every inch of the way, we'll make it. *To Nome.*

Cresting Cape Nome

28

A Line Dance

Iditarod day 13: Beyond Safety

Safety is an old roadhouse that sits on a narrow spit of land. It's the final Iditarod checkpoint—so close to Nome that mushers rarely rest there, although during the race's history a few have scratched in Safety when tired dogs have refused to move on. Greg tells me that during training runs the roadhouse is his customary feeding place; now he offers his dogs a light meal. Meanwhile I worry that mine might never move again.

Greg understands. He encourages me to go ahead, but that's another kind of gamble. I'm pretty sure the trail crosses sea ice between here and Nome. There is also something plain wrong about finishing ahead of this saint who has gotten us through the last fifty miles. No, we'll follow him in. That's exactly as it should be. So I dole out lamb snacks, change some booties, and fluff up the dogs while Greg's dogs lick their bowls clean.

When we're ready to leave, the checker hands me my starting bib, which I'd handed to the volunteers in Yentna Station, the first checkpoint of the race. "Here you go, Debbie. Remember, you need to have it on when you finish," he tells me.

When you finish.

The words replay in my mind as I pull the bib over my head. Clipping its buckles makes me stand a few inches taller.

Then, in the muted light of dawn, Greg's dogs are eager to leave. So are mine. Juliet noses Sydney. Reno and Spur bound ahead—as do Topaz and Spot. Zeppy prances, towering above Snickers and Fang who motor along in wheel. Meanwhile, I stand with both feet on the drag to slow them and keep them from passing. Greg turns and shakes his head, watching my spunky team chasing. Again he encourages me to go by.

"Really, it's okay. You should," he tells me.

Once more I decline, explaining that he is my hero and that we would follow him anywhere. "Well, at least to Nome," I add.

The truth is that I'm tempted to pass. These are the last twenty-two miles of our epic adventure—miles to be intimately savored between musher and dogs. I've always imagined running them alone here with no one else nearby; I wonder if Greg feels the same way. He keeps the option alive.

"Just let me know," he calls with a smile. "Your dogs are looking pretty perky."

Sometime later—maybe an hour—we're still trotting behind Greg. Off to the side the sky is light pink giving way to aqua. Overhead it boasts dawn's deepest blue. We've just taken a right turn away from the shore, and ahead is a wide-open hill etched with a straight line: the trail. From studying photos before the race, I recognize that we're looking at 675-foot-high Cape Nome. We're ten miles from the finish.

At the base of the cape, Greg sets both his snow hooks. "I'm going to stop and snack them here, Debbie. They expect it. Really, go on."

This time I agree to give it a try, adding something about owing him thanks for the rest of my lifetime. "On by!" I call. "On by!"

My voice is scratchy, but Sydney and Juliet share my celebratory spirit. They zip past Greg and scamper up the long, gradual slope. I'm so elated, I get off my sled to run alongside it. After ten steps I'm coughing and gasping, my legs burning with marathon cramps. I'm laughing at myself as I stumble back onto the runners. I ride only long enough to recover. Then I leap off to run some more.

Cresting the cape is one of those moments composed of magic: nine dogs zip ahead of me, their crimson coats brilliant in the promising light of morning. The hillside is snow-covered and gentle. In my memory there's not a tree in sight. Just my huskies surging over pristine white hills beneath a salmon sky and the dark blue sea in the distance. I'm riding with one foot on the sled runner, the other pedaling the snow. My dogs and I move in harmony, their rhythm pulsing through the line to my own. We're in a line dance, one that we know by heart.

The artistry of our shared momentum consumes me, but at the same time I understand that this dance, like all others, will end. This grace will fade and give way to inevitable stumbles. That's the way it is. The present is what matters, this moment gifted from them. From spritely Juliet and coy Sydney leading, with their ears erect and their necks held high. Reno and Spur in swing, their elegant tails floating behind. Next Topaz and Spot trotting to the tempo like they did when I struggled over the steps and the gorge, one thousand miles ago. Then Zeppy running solo, his laid-back hound-dog gait suggesting he's known all along that this time would come. Wheelers Fang and Snickers charging in front of me—trotting to the tempo, steady and true.

A snow machine buzzes nearby. The humming grows louder, and a man pulls alongside us, waving. He stops to take photos. I smile as we pass him and hope to see the pictures someday. He cheers and speeds off, leaving us surging past Iditarod markers and some fences. Maybe a gate. Somewhere there's a building. Then a few cars. Someone waves and honks the horn. The trail leads to a road crossing where there's a cluster of people, including a woman wearing pink flannel pajamas.

I recognize her: DeeDee Jonrowe. She's an accomplished Iditarod veteran who's claimed several near wins and endured a devastating scratch. She's also a two-year breast cancer survivor who will never give in to life's setbacks. Now, after claiming tenth place, DeeDee has gotten out of bed on a Sunday morning to cheer for me. She yells congratulations, and then she tells me to go straight across the road and down a hill to the beach.

"We don't go back onto the ice, do we?" I ask, choking on one last miserable thought.

"Oh yes you do," she says, laughing, "but don't you worry. You're going to be just fine!"

Down we charge to the frozen sea, toward a few markers set in a white frozen expanse. The burled arch may be close, but we're not there yet.

The team lopes onto the ice. The sled skitters, and so does everything inside me. I don't dare say one word to the dogs—and within a few elongated seconds I know that all is well. Juliet and Sydney hold a spunky pace. They and the others charge on.

We're cruising close to shore when I first hear it: the siren rising. This time the ringing doesn't evoke memories of civil defense drills or the chilling wail of an ambulance. It calls something I've never heard before.

"This one is for you!" I cry to the dogs. "For us!" I claim.

I've always wondered how the end of the race would feel and envisioned stopping the dogs on the outskirts of Nome in order to share one last Iditarod moment. Pausing here for a celebratory snack is tempting, but momentum is all that matters. That much I've learned. So I simply call out each name as we cruise up a bluff to the street. *The* street. Front Street, Nome.

"Straight ahead, Juliet and Sydney, straight ahead!" I call. "Good girl, Spur. Good boy, Reno."

They bound over a dwindling ribbon of snow, down the center of the asphalt road. Together we move past legendary bars and clapboard houses built during the gold rush. My dogs run where huskies of history have carried mail and serum and desperately needed supplies to this Arctic community isolated in winter.

This mile brings back others, and my own history overtakes me. Salt and I are slipping through spruce trees in the moonlight above Anchorage, in four inches of fresh snow. That moment blends into another. I'm with Hannah and Salt as they complete their first one-dog race. Then I'm crossing the two-dog finish with Andy and Moxie and Morgan. Now we're cruising down the street of Andy's Iditarod triumph. We're waving to the crowd the way Mark did one year ago.

The past inspires and informs. It's always with us, but to look down Front Street from the runners of my dogsled is a sight that has everything yet nothing to do with what has come before. This moment is the culmination of a two-thousand-mile double adventure, the messy beauty of its struggle, and the ultimate surrender to the fact that some endings are happy and others are not.

And now: the burled arch.

I see it, one short block away. Juliet noses Sydney, and my spicy nine-dog team scampers up the snowy ramp, underneath the arch, and across the legendary line. We are 2005 Iditarod Finishers: Juliet, Sydney, Reno, Spur, Spot, Topaz, Zeppy, Fang, Snickers. And me.

I set my hook and look up to a circle of smiling faces. Among many are Mark and Andy and Hannah. My sister, Vicky. One tight hug and another. Mark Nordman. Jeff King. Vern Halter. Martin Buser. And beaming, windburnt Mel.

The mayor of Nome approaches with a sign-in clipboard. I scribble my name and listen as he announces our finish. "Debbie Moderow, I am pleased to announce you have officially completed the 2005 Iditarod Trail Sled Dog Race in thirteen days, nineteen hours, ten minutes, and fifty-two seconds. Welcome to Nome."

The proclamation is nice, but the formality pulls me away from the dogs. So I work my way past the handshakes and hugs, the smiles and the congratulatory words—to be with them.

My huskies love finish line celebrations; they've been granted more than a few. As I pat and thank each one, they wag their tails and roll in the snow. Then they gobble pieces of salmon and herring doled out by Andy and Hannah. My dogs show no hint of their moody shenanigans, and they're certainly not tired. Juliet rubs her back against Sydney, and Reno's afraid of the crowd. Zeppy's eyeing his harness as if he's about to chew it. Topaz leans against my sister, who strokes her, while Spur de-booties her front paws.

I linger with them, trying to trust that we've come to an ending, to that long-sought place where the high stakes of adventure can rest. But that's not how they see it. Spot sounds the first woof and gives the gang line a tug. Then Zeppy paws the snow. Sydney leans into a happy dog stretch, while Juliet circles behind and gives her a pounce. A yip and a yowl blend with a few more, and soon they're all tugging on the line, ready to run.

My dogs are not confused. They're not thinking we're at a race start, or leaving a checkpoint to cross a restless river in the night. Some of them might even recognize Nome and understand that they've passed through the shade of the arch—that a few blocks ahead is the Iditarod dog yard, where they'll eat a big meal and bed down on huge flakes of straw.

I can never know exactly what they're thinking. That's the reality that distinguishes us and defines the mystery that draws us together as one. At this moment my nine huskies are jubilant. And so am I. They look to me with bright eyes that are weathered, wise, and true. Right now, in the light of a clear-sky Bering Sea morning, they insist it is time to move on.

Juliet and Sydney, Iditarod Finishers, holding out
the team under the arch

Epilogue

Our finish line celebration on that brilliant March morning was joyful like no other, but it didn't last long. When my huskies clamored to go, I agreed to leave the burled arch behind.

The winter that followed brought change to many of my Iditarod Finishers. Taiga found her way to a new home, complete with a couch and a devoted family who took her skiing and hiking for the better part of a decade. Wolf and Roulette became stars in a small recreational kennel. Mark and I delivered Fang and Creek to a loving retired couple in upstate New York. Strider joined a junior team that specialized in her favorite activity: running short, fast miles. Every farewell brought me sorrow and nostalgia for the trail, but I believed in the promise of each pairing. After all, Salt had shown us that life for a retired sled dog is full of reward.

While striving to secure the best future for each Salty Dog elder, I grappled with a disturbing challenge: Kanga. As much as I loathed the reality, I recognized that she was not a positive player on our dog team. Her alpha moody persona worked against the sensitive and earnest spirit of the others. I knew she should not run with our huskies again.

This truth wore me down, and the dog did not make it easy. From the moment I returned home from Iditarod, Kanga tracked every move of mine with that look of complete devotion. When I took her for hikes in summertime, she streaked over tundra with effortless agility, then returned to me for a biscuit. At mealtime in the dog yard she insisted on extra pats, and I responded with genuine affection. We had always had a special bond. That would never change.

In the end, Mark and I decided to keep her for a while longer—and to breed her with our happy-go-lucky male, Terry Kern. We had bred only a few litters over the years, believing that professional mushers were best suited to improve sled dog genetics. But Kanga and Terry Kern both came from renowned bloodlines proven by Iditarod champions. By combining her talent and smarts with his straightforward tail-wagging disposition, we hoped for the best of both.

We were not disappointed. We treated Kanga like royalty while she raised a mighty litter of eight; those honest pups have led us on a variety of trails ever since. Eventually, we chose a retirement kennel for Kanga. We subjected several good friends to weeks of intense questioning before choosing an owner for Kanga who promised to give her exceptional love and care for the rest of her days.

A few seasons later, when Kanga's pups turned one, Mark, Hannah, and I embarked again on the long trail from Nenana to Nome, this time as part of the 2007 Norman Vaughan Serum Run Expedition. Mark rode a snow machine in support, while Hannah and I mushed the eight-hundred-mile route. My younger Iditarod Finishers—Sydney, Juliet, Spot, Lightning, Zeppy, Spur, and Topaz—grounded our teams with their wisdom. Along the way they mentored Kanga's eight yearlings.

When Hannah and I first schemed about the Serum Run, I envisioned retracing my legendary miles on a mellow mother-daughter journey. Traveling a mere forty miles a day would offer the perfect chance to teach the youngsters to lead. No longer bound by Iditarod's clock, Mark, Hannah, and I could sleep every night and travel at a relaxed pace in daylight. We could visit with children in the villages. Above all, the Serum Run would be a dog fest, a trip across Alaska with my daughter and husband. Together we'd have time to relax with our huskies into each unfolding mile.

I should have known better.

From the start in Nenana, temperatures were bitter cold, twenty degrees below zero. But at least this time we didn't have to worry about open water. Our expedition, which included twelve dog teams and at least as many snow machiners, launched onto a river locked in thick ice. The weather that day was manageable, but by the time we reached Manley, my thermometer recorded minus fifty degrees. For the next ten days, all the way to Kaltag, we pushed through the Yukon's deepest cold.

At first our large group struggled to adjust. Conditions were harsh, demanding vigilance in caring for ourselves, our dogs, and one another. Out on the trail, Hannah and I ran in sight of each other. We crossed Fish Lake in daylight, and this time we spent three full days camping on the long haul between Tanana and Ruby. When temperatures on the Yukon plummeted to minus sixty, we took our time making certain everyone stayed safe. We'd been on the trail for two full weeks when we left Kaltag for Unalakleet. This time when we passed the original Old Woman cabin, I tossed her a cookie. I was counting on her good favor.

Our miles on the coast began well. In the continuing cold, Hannah and I ran close together, cheering our huskies and each other past the shelter cabin and my own ghosts on the ice. Kanga's pups ran that day with noticeable spunk. Spicy like their mother but always eager, they moved along toward Koyuk with unusual confidence. Soon after we reached Elim, the temperature rose to a balmy minus ten degrees. We set out the next morning toward White Mountain in the highest of spirits, never guessing that our biggest challenge would soon come. The crux of our Serum Run journey took place on Golovin Bay.

Mark and some other snow machiners had gone ahead that morning. They were waiting for us outside of the village of Golovin, at the start of the eighteen-mile crossing. It was minus twenty degrees and blowing a furious gale when they waved us to a stop on the edge of the bay. Peering through frozen goggles, Mark checked my face and Hannah's for frostbite and asked if we needed any help. He explained that we could stay in Golovin, but there would be much better shelter at White Mountain. Hannah and I both were doing okay, and our teams were eager. We elected to toss the dogs a fat snack and continue. My history on the coast told me to keep moving. I also knew that the wind was not our friend.

My team went first, with Juliet and Sydney in lead. Hannah followed close behind us, running Spur and Lightning up front. To travel with my very capable daughter, each of us with seven or eight dogs, felt like a reasonable plan. There was safety in the buddy system, and after all, the bay was only eighteen miles long. Our huskies would be fine, in their arctic coats trimmed with fur. Hannah and I donned multiple layers proven to protect us. I had done this all before.

Armed with these reassuring notions, we headed onto the ice. After the first mile or so Mark passed us on his machine, and we gave him the "all good" signal—but sometime in the next few miles the wind increased, delivering a punch more intense than any I'd experienced before. Knives of cold sliced through zippers on my anorak and snowsuit; every gust cast a chill that burned anything exposed.

The temperature was brutal, but the wind was our nemesis that day. Furious gusts sent our sleds skittering sideways on black ice; Hannah and I struggled to help our teams stay on the marked course. The whistling gale screamed fair warning: we had to keep moving. Yet, from Iditarod I knew that sometimes dogs say no. Sometimes they have the final word.

That afternoon our huskies said yes. Sydney and Juliet trudged onward, inspiring the youngsters behind them. Across miles of black ice striped with white drifts, they pushed into one agitated gust and another. This time my dog team and I collaborated, giving every mile all that we had. Every so often Mark appeared, and we waved him on. Whenever I looked back at Hannah's team, I saw dark dog eyes peering through white masks of snow—and huskies trudging onward. Behind them my daughter pedaled, giving the dogs some help.

After several intense hours, we passed a single spruce tree crooked from the wind; I knew we were off the ice and that the worst was behind us. Juliet must have known also. She nosed Sydney and leapt forward, like she wanted to play tag. For another half hour they pressed on.

Then my huskies stopped.

It was snowing so hard, I couldn't see why. When I set my hooks and looked up, Mark stood alongside me. "You've made it," he said. "We're in White Mountain."

At first I didn't believe him. There was no visibility, no view of the buildings on top of the bluff. No sign of any other teams or their snow machiners. I'd been in this exact place before, but swirls of white concealed the landmarks in my memory.

As Hannah parked her team behind me, I walked up the line praising each dog. Then I huddled with my leaders on the ground. Sydney and Juliet had never hesitated during those brutal miles. This crossing belonged to them. I thanked them and trembled, chilled with fright for where we'd traveled. Sydney responded by leaning close, while Juliet crawled into my lap. Wiping their faces clean, I thanked them again. Together we'd finished another race, this one against the elements—a contest I did not choose. Despite our vulnerability, we trusted one another. We made it through.

You'd think I would have reveled in the glory of my team's performance while I sat on the snow with my leaders—their achievement was nothing short of magnificent—but I was shaken. My pride in having triumphed where we'd previously stumbled, was overcome by my understanding that we were lucky. If the wind had whipped any harder, or if one young dog had grown disheartened, we might not have been able to continue.

After navigating thousands of Iditarod miles with my huskies, I had changed. To have scratched from one race and finished another no longer signified the difference between failure and success. Our ability to negotiate those exposed miles of Golovin Bay did not simply prove that we could prevail where we had stumbled before. Instead, I recognized that during that crossing we had traveled a precarious line—no different from many of life's trajectories. We'd done well, but in my father's words, the ball might have taken a cockeyed bounce.

Maybe Dad understood this all along. He lived his years reaching for glory with passion, humility, and grit. From fighting on the front lines of a devastating war to witnessing the birth of his unlikely third child, and everything in between, my father gave every day on this earth all that he had. Still, he believed that the biggest triumphs—life's moments of grace—are never purely deserved.

As I huddled with Juliet and Sydney in White Mountain, I understood for the first time that to cherish our crossing of Golovin Bay, or any of life's thresholds, was to trust the messy authenticity of doing the best that we can. To revel in the glory of that particular destination was to honor my huskies: their athletic brilliance and their resilient hearts, as well as their infuriating weaknesses—and, yes, my own.

Aware of a call for resilience, I focused on caring for my dogs in White Mountain. After taking off booties and ladling out a warm meal, I dug a deep hole in the snow for each husky and filled each crater with straw. These sheltered nests drew instant approval: each wagging friend sniffed and circled before settling in. When everyone was content and curled nose-to-tail, I returned to Juliet and Sydney. I'd made them a double nest in the lee of my sled. I massaged Sydney's wrists and then reached for Juliet, wanting to offer my leader, who hates the cold, some extra love.

With my own teeth chattering, I stroked her wet little mouse face. She nibbled on my gloves, then wriggled out of my arms and pawed at my sled. She wanted her sleeping bag.

Of course she did.

I pulled it out and opened it wide. She dove in.

Anything for her, and the others.

Always.

Acknowledgments

All photos courtesy of the Moderow family, with the following exceptions: Doug Sonerholm: page vi, Debbie with Juliet and Sydney, winter 2005; page 44, Training run, winter 2005; page 186, Nearing the starting line, Iditarod 2005; page 208, Cruising with the 2005 team; page 232, Juliet in her sleeping bag; page 277, Juliet and Sydney, Iditarod finishers, holding out the team under the arch; Brian T. Smith: page 2, Ready to go; Patrick Endres: page 6, Kanga and Juliet lead Debbie and team onto the 2003 Iditarod Trail; Bert Morgan Archive: page 18, Do Clarke in her autogiro; Jim Hale: page 34, Debbie and Mark skiing on the Ruth Glacier, summer 1979; Anchorage Daily News/Bill Roth: page 56, Debbie skijoring with Charlotte and Salt, winter 1990; Charles Mason: page 144, Debbie and Sydney; page 164, Debbie joking around with Kanga; Dennis Cowals: page 182, Debbie and her dad before her wedding ceremony, 1980; Bryan Imus: page 270, Cresting Cape Nome.

In Gratitude

There is an uncanny resemblance between running the Iditarod Trail Sled Dog Race and completing a memoir. Both projects require passion, dedication to learning, and an immense amount of patience; each undertaking requires the collaboration of many beating hearts. In the midst of each journey, I questioned the wisdom of taking on such a project and wondered if it would ever come to conclusion. While running Iditarod and writing this memoir, I have vacillated between daring and doubt.

Fast into the Night is the continuation of my Iditarod adventure. I could not have pushed toward Nome without my talented leaders: Juliet, Sydney, Kanga, Reno, Spur, Taiga, and Lil' Su. We would not have undertaken those long miles if a white dog named Salt had never walked through our door. He was the founder of our family's Salty Dog Kennel.

To compare my human mentors to my leaders on the trail is no casual conceit. Alaskan writers Andromeda Romano-Lax, Lee Goodman, and Bill Sherwonit pulled me through the earliest awkward writing miles. Scott Russell Sanders heightened my commitment to the long literary trail.

Ultimately, Judith Kitchen and Stan Rubin, directors and founders of Pacific Lutheran University's Rainier Writing Workshop, drew me into an MFA program that made all the difference. Mentors Gary Ferguson, Brenda Miller, and Dinah Lenney guided me into a stunning and challenging literary topography. Agent Elizabeth Kaplan greeted me into the publishing world with a hearty welcome and precise navigational skill. Houghton Mifflin Harcourt editor Susan Canavan, from our first conversation, honored my dogs by holding me to her high standards. The skilled and generous people of Red Hen Press, including Kate Gale, Peggy Shumaker, and Hannah Moye, facilitated the release of the 2018 softcover edition.

To Mark and Andy and Hannah: this is our story. Together, and on separate trails, we have all embarked with our dogs into the magnificent Alaskan night. First we fell in love with a bunch of backyard huskies. Then we dared and inspired one another to set our sights on a distant horizon. Finally we helped one another travel by dog team toward Nome.

I thank Hannah, talented writer and the first MFA graduate in our family, for daring me to attend graduate school. Her writing companionship has delivered timeless, thorough, and detailed editorial wisdom. To Andy I am grateful for the handoff of an Iditarod legacy—and also for ever-honest and feisty responses to many drafts of this story. My deepest gratitude goes to Mark, for his love and dedication, which has enabled me to tackle one daring and all-consuming adventure, and then another.

Biographical Note

Author photo by Mike Conti

Debbie Clarke Moderow has lived in Alaska for thirty-eight years. In 1977 she graduated with a BA from Princeton University, and in 2013 she earned an MFA in Creative Writing from Pacific Lutheran University's Rainier Writing Workshop. She ran the Iditarod in 2003 and 2005, finishing the 2005 race in thirteen days, nineteen hours, ten minutes, and fifty-two seconds. Her memoir *Fast into the Night* received the 2016 National Outdoor Book Award in Outdoor Literature and the 2017 WILLA Award in Creative Nonfiction.